# SOCIAL CARE AND THE LAW

## An NVQ Related Reference Guide for Direct Care Staff

By: Siobhan Maclean
and Mark Shiner

Kirwin Maclean Associates Ltd

City & Guilds name and logo are the registered trade marks of the City and Guilds of London Institute and are used under licence.

"City and Guilds logo © City & Guilds 2002"

Social Care and the Law: An NVQ Related Reference Guide

First published 1999 by Kirwin Maclean Associates
First Edition 1999: ISBN: 0-9534083-1-0
Second Edition 1999: ISBN: 0-934083-2-9
Third Edition 1999: ISBN: 0-9534083-3-7
Fourth Edition 2000: ISBN: 0-953408-7-X
Fifth Edition 2000: ISBN: 1-903575-03-6
Sixth Edition 2001: ISBN: 1-903575-10-9
Seventh Edition 2001: ISBN: 1-903575-14-1
Eighth Edition 2003: ISBN: 1-903575-23-0
Ninth Edition 2005: ISBN: 1-903575-30-3
Tenth Edition 2005: ISBN: 1-903575-34-6
Eleventh Edition 2006: ISBN: 978-1-903575-45-1
**Twelfth Edition 2008: ISBN: 978-1-903575-54-3**

A catalogue record for this book will be available from the British Library.

©Kirwin Maclean Associates Ltd, 47 Albion Street, Rugeley, Staffs
All rights Reserved

ISBN: 978-1-903575-54-3
Printed in Great Britain by Kirwin Maclean Associates Ltd

# CONTENTS

# INTRODUCTION

Direct care staff are expected to have a knowledge of the legal and legislative framework within which they work.

Many care staff are now working towards National Vocational Qualifications (NVQs) in Health and Social Care, which specify the knowledge a worker needs to have in order to carry out their work. Many of the knowledge specifications make reference to the worker's need to have an understanding of legislation relevant to their work.

This book is intended to act as a reference point for direct care staff, NVQ assessors and managers. All of the legislation and some national policy initiatives relevant to social care work with adults is outlined briefly. It is not intended, however, to equip the reader with detailed specific knowledge on either the legal system or on specific legal points. Each section makes reference to relevant NVQ units to aid easy reference for NVQ candidates and assessors.

The law is constantly changing and we therefore advise you to be aware that the contents of this book are correct at the time of writing. Where changes in the law are expected we have highlighted this.

We would strongly advise you to encourage your manager to ensure that you have access to the relevant texts of the major pieces of legislation relevant to your workplace.

# 1  THE BRITISH LEGAL FRAMEWORK

It is worth having some idea of the way that law comes about. There are a number of different types of "legislation" – including Acts, Regulations etc and a clear relationship between policy and legislation. This chapter will help to clarify these issues.

It should be noted that British law involves four countries (England, Wales, Scotland and Northern Ireland). The Scottish legal system is very different to that of England and Wales. On the whole, the legal framework of Northern Ireland is very similar to the English and Welsh framework.

Most legislation is the result of an Act of Parliament. This is usually introduced by the Government of the day and voted upon within the two Houses of Parliament, often being amended as it goes through. At this point it is called a Bill. A Bill becomes an Act once it has passed through Parliament and been given Royal Assent.

Generally a number of stages are gone through before a Government introduces proposed legislation to Parliament. These stages form part of a period of proposal and consultation. This usually starts with what is known as a *Green Paper* - a paper which the Government puts out in order to test public opinion. An example is the Green Paper "Independence, Well-being and Choice: Our Vision for the future of Social Care for Adults in England" - published in 2005.

Alternatively, the Government can ask a committee or an individual to produce a report following research and investigation into the area in question. For example, The Griffiths Report proposed the structure of community care which was ultimately laid down in the NHS and Community Care Act 1990.

Following the Green Paper a *White Paper* is often published. This is a statement of what the proposed legislation will cover. It usually lays out the philosophy and general principles of the legislation. It is important to be clear that not all Green Papers are followed by a White Paper and not all White Papers lead to an Act of Parliament. An example of a White Paper which was not followed up by an Act of Parliament is "Valuing People: A New Strategy for Learning Disability for the 21$^{st}$ Century" which was published in 2001.

However, not all Acts of Parliament are proposed by the Government. Some start off as *Private Members Bills*. These are introduced into Parliament by individual MPs. One example of this is the Carers Equal Opportunities Act 2004.

Acts of Parliament sometimes contain powers which allow the Government to introduce the Act over a period of time. Therefore just because an Act has been passed it does not necessarily mean that everything in it is current law. For Example, the Human Rights Act 1998 was not implemented until October 2000, a full two years after it received Royal Assent. Much of The Disabled Person's (Services, Consultation and representation) Act 1986 was never implemented.

Acts of Parliament often include a clause which gives the senior minister involved (usually called the Secretary of State) the power to introduce regulations at a later date. These regulations detail more specific law on areas covered by the Act. This is done by means of Statutory Instrument which goes before Parliament but is not usually debated. An example of this is the Mental Capacity Act 2005 which is supplemented by later regulations. The Care Standards Act 2000 provided the Secretary of State with the power to make regulations relating to requirements that care homes must meet, eg: The Care Homes Regulations 2001.

Since devolution, the Welsh Assembly Government has had the power and responsibility to make regulations to support Acts that have gone through Westminster. Often therefore there are regulations that cover a very similar area of practice but the English and Welsh regulations are specific to their own home country. Wherever possible we have made clear the national differences but staff working in Wales are advised to check with their employer about the exact regulations they work under. In a book of this size, it is not always possible to give an overview of all relevant regulations and guidance.

In addition, the Secretary of State for Health has the general power to issue guidance to local authorities. Local authorities are under a legal duty to follow this guidance. This guidance may be related to an Act or may be in response to situations that have arisen. For example, the guidance relating to protecting vulnerable adults from abuse is not linked to any specific Act.

In addition, major pieces of law may be followed at a later date by Codes of Practice. These do not have the same force of law, but they explain and clarify the law and offer guidance on expected practice. They should therefore be followed by practitioners.

Whilst some major pieces of legislation encompass all areas and replace all previous Acts, very often new legislation amends previous Acts of Parliament, creating increasing complexity. For example, the Mental Health Act 2007 amends, rather than replaces, the Mental Health Act 1983. We have noted in this book where Acts amend other previous legislation.

Staff need to be aware that policy is also a major factor in the way services develop. In many ways, legislation is only one of the ways that policy can be pursued and applied. Other ways that policy can be pursued are by the Government making additional money available if certain targets are met or through the relevant department exercising a leadership role. In origin, the Surestart initiative and Children's Centres were all fuelled by money. It is a number of years since the initiative started and only now has legislation been enacted to 'confirm' the initiative. On the whole local authorities and NHS authorities are under a duty to follow the directions sent out by the relevant Government department.

It should be clear by this stage that "Law" therefore, covers a range of areas. In addition to this, there is case law – where a case is taken to a court, the court may make a judgement which interprets the law and sets a precedent.

Having a clear understanding of "the law" is therefore about more than knowing about Acts of Parliament – as the following diagram shows the range of legislation.

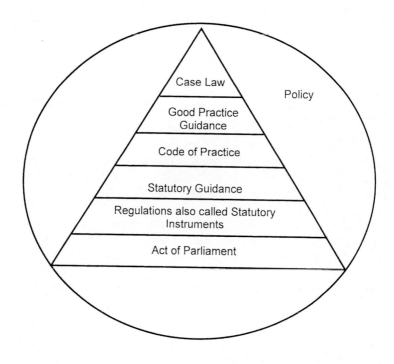

We have tried to cover a range of the different types of legislation in this book. Examples of each 'layer' include:

O   Acts of Parliament – one example is The Mental Capacity Act 2005. We have tried to cover all the relevant Acts of Parliament in this book. We have also detailed a few Bills which are currently going through Parliament.

O   Regulations – one example would be employment equality regulations – a number of which are covered in Chapter 4.

O   Statutory Guidance – an example would include Fair Access to Care Services: Guidance on eligibility criteria for adult social care, published in 2002.

O   Code of Practice – The Mental Health Act 1983 has an associated Code of Practice. The Care Standards Act 2000 places a responsibility on the GSCC to issue a code of practice for social care workers. Codes of Practice are referred to where relevant in the book.

O   Good Practice Guidance – the Government issues a range of good practice guidance which changes regularly. Since there is so much good practice guidance, we have not covered this in the book but staff should make sure that they are familiar with the good practice guidance relevant to their area of practice.

O   Case Law – one example of the impact of case law is the way that the Bournewood Judgement led to the Mental Health Act 2007 amending the Mental Capacity Act 2005.

O   Policy – the Government has published a range of documents which demonstrate that their current major policy drive is what has become known as the "personalisation agenda".

 **In Summary**

This background information is offered to provide you with an understanding of the legislative framework within which you operate. It is not important for you to know about the detail of the complex English and Welsh legal system but a basic understanding will help you to recognise the framework from which the law arises.

# EUROPEAN LEGISLATION

The knowledge specification for the Health and Social Care NVQs states that the staff member needs to know, understand and apply current local, national and European legislation. The inclusion of the reference to European legislation has caused a great deal of uncertainty for assessors and anxiety for NVQ candidates.

This chapter should help to clarify issues around European legislation.

Member states of the European Union (EU) have agreed that EU directives, in various subject areas, have to be applied to member states' own laws. Areas in which the EU has the legislative lead, through directives, include:

O   employment law and workers rights (especially equality of opportunity)

O   health and safety in the workplace

O   business activities and trade

O   consumer rights

O   free movement of labour across the EU

O   aspects of public health (communicable diseases)

The EU requires that member states translate their Directives into the member states own national laws. The exact wording of the national laws is up to each member state but the shared objectives must be achieved. Member states MUST translate the Directives within certain timescales or face enforcement action from the EU – usually successive official 'telling offs' with the final sanction being a fine applied by the European Court of Justice, (which applies EU law to all member states). It is only in exceptional circumstances that an individual citizen of a member state could invoke an EU directive directly.

In terms of the health and social care sector, the main impact of EU Directives has been to introduce changes to health and safety law, employment law and laws relating to countering discrimination. Examples of EU Directives that have resulted in changes to British law include:

O   Health and Safety at Work Directive (89/391/EEC) (Framework) resulted in the introduction of the Management of Health and Safety at Work Regulations 1992 (since amended).

O   EU Directive 90/268/EEC (Manual Handling of Loads) resulted in the introduction of the Manual Handling Operations Regulations 1992

O   EU Directive 89/654/EEC (Workplaces) resulted in the introduction of the Workplace (Health, Safety and Welfare) Regulations 1992

O  EU Directive 2000/43/EC (Racial Equality) resulted in the introduction of the Race Relations Act 1976 (Amendment) Regulations 2003

O  EU Directive 2000/78/EC (Equal Treatment in Employment) has resulted in the:

   - Employment Equality (Sexual Orientation) Regulations 2003
   - Disability Discrimination Act 1995 (Amendment) Regulations 2003
   - Employment Equality (Age) Regulations 2006

O  EU Directive 2002/73/EC (Equal Treatment for Men and Women in Employment and Training) has resulted in the Employment Equality (Sex Discrimination) Regulations 2005

### In Summary

Where a unit knowledge specification makes reference to European legislation and/or directives, it is sufficient within the UK to refer to Westminster legislation – as covered in this book.  There is no need for you to look any wider since all relevant European legislation will have been translated into British law by Parliament.

# 3  THE COURT SYSTEM IN ENGLAND AND WALES

In considering the legal system, it is always useful to have an understanding of the court system. Generally speaking there are two distinct Court systems in England and Wales. One covering criminal cases and one dealing with civil matters.

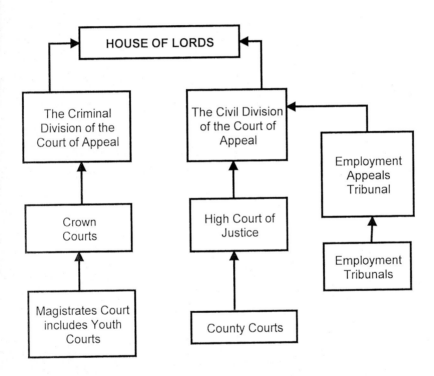

This chapter gives a brief outline of the different courts in this system.

## Magistrates Courts

These are sometimes known as the "Court of first instance". Essentially, they are the lowest of the Courts in England and Wales. They deal principally with criminal matters and the jurisdiction of the Magistrates is limited. Therefore, they deal predominantly with less serious offences or they refer people on to Crown Court.

## Youth Courts

The 1991 Criminal Justice Act renamed the old Juvenile Courts and Juvenile Court Panels as "Youth Courts" and "Youth Court Panels". The Youth Court was given something of a procedural makeover with the presiding magistrates given specific training. The Youth Court deals with young people up to and including the age of 17.

## Crown Courts

These deal with more serious criminal cases and appeals from Magistrates Courts. They involve a judge and jury and are the traditional view of Courts.

## County Courts

These Courts act as the first point of call for civil cases. They operate on an area basis and are normally presided over by circuit judges or registrars.

## High Court of Justice

This Court deals with more high profile and complex civil matters. Cases here are heard by a High Court Judge. There are three divisions of the High Court.

a) The Queens Bench – this division deals with issues of contract and supervises lower Courts and tribunals.
b) The Chancery Division – this division deals with a range of matters including wills and bankruptcy.
c) The Family Division – this division deals with family matters e.g.: divorce matters, matters relating to children etc.

## Court of Appeal

This Court has two divisions:

a) Civil – this hears appeals from County Courts and the High Court of Justice.
b) Criminal – this hears appeals from the Crown Court.

## The House of Lords

The House of Lords hears appeals on important legal issues from the Court of Appeal and (rarely) from the High Court. These issues are heard by the Law Lords.

## Tribunals

In addition to the Court system outlined there are also a variety of employment tribunals. Tribunals deal with a range of employment issues including those involving industrial relations, equal pay and sex discrimination. They consist of a legally qualified chairperson (appointed by the Lord Chancellor) and two lay members – one from a managerial background and one from a trade union.

 ### In Summary

It is not important to have a detailed understanding of the court system but it is always useful to place an understanding of legislation into the context of the Court system.

# 4  ANTI-OPPRESSIVE PRACTICE

## Introduction

In Great Britain we have a history of legislation designed to ensure that discrimination on certain grounds is unlawful. It is important to know about this legislation and to develop an understanding of the way in which this applies to your work setting.

It is also important to have a clear understanding of the legislative framework in order to enhance your own practice in terms of combating oppression. However, be warned that good practice is way ahead of the minimum legal requirements.

If you think of anti-oppressive practice as a bag of tools then the legal framework is one tool to aid your practice. There are two other good reasons to be aware of what the law says in this area – firstly, you are required to work within the law. Secondly, you need to be aware of what action could be taken if any of the people you work with have been oppressed and wish to take legal action.

There are a number of pieces of legislation relevant to this area. This chapter will cover:

- Sex Discrimination Act (SDA) 1975
- Equal Pay Act 1970/1975
- Race Relations Act (RRA) 1976
- NHS and Community Care Act 1990
- Disability Discrimination Act 1995.
- Race Relations (Amendment) Act 2000
- Disability Discrimination Act 2005
- Equality Act 2006

and associated regulations

## Sex Discrimination Act 1975

Definitions of discrimination are vital in terms of understanding and operating this piece of legislation. This Act makes it unlawful to discriminate on the grounds of gender. Discrimination is set out into two forms – direct and indirect.

*Direct Discrimination* is quite straightforward. Simply stated it means that one person is treated less favourably than another based on gender. If a woman, for example, is treated less favourably than a man because of typical, stereotyped views about the role of women in society, that could amount to direct discrimination. One example of this would be if a woman is refused a pint of bitter in a public house and told that they only serve half pints to women.

*Indirect Discrimination* is more complex. It takes place if a requirement or condition is imposed which, on the face of it, is nothing to do with gender but in practice is such that, for example, the proportion of women who can comply with it is considerably less than the proportion of men who can comply with it. For example, a height requirement for a job may be classed as indirect discrimination if it would exclude women from applying.

The Sex Discrimination Act also makes it unlawful to discriminate on the ground of marital status.

As a result of various European Union Directives, the Sex Discrimination Act 1975 has been progressively amended. The Employment Equality (Sex Discrimination) Regulations 2005 have made various changes including:

O  harassment, including sexual harassment, on the grounds of a person's gender is made unlawful

O  discrimination on the grounds of pregnancy or maternity leave is classified as unlawful sex discrimination

The Equality Act 2006 inserted a general duty on public authorities into the 1975 Act. This new duty is:

O  in carrying out their functions, public authorities must have due regard to the need

- to eliminate unlawful discrimination and harassment
- promote equality of opportunity between men and women

A number of statutory exemptions apply under the Act – for example, charitable bodies are able to confer benefits on members of one sex only.

The Act does allow for positive action. For example, where being of a particular sex is a genuine occupational qualification. Positive action may, for example, mean advertising for a male member of staff to work with men where personal care is involved. This Act also set up the Equal Opportunities Commission, which has since been replaced by the Commission for Equality and Human Rights.

**The Sex Discrimination Act 1975 (Public Authorities) (Statutory Duties) Order 2006 (Ref: 2006 No. 2930)**
**With effect from 6th April 2006**

The 1975 Sex Discrimination Act was amended by the Equality Act 2006 which, by inserting new sections 76a to 76e, imposed a general duty on public authorities to eliminate unlawful discrimination, including harassment, when carrying out their functions. This Order establishes the Gender Equality Duty Code of Practice imposed by the Secretary of State and prepared by the Equal Opportunities Commission. The EOC has since been replaced by the Commission for Equality and Human Rights (CEHR).

Essentially, the Code of Practice requires public authorities to carry out certain gender equality duties which centre around three main requirements. Public Authorities must:

O   Draw up, publish and review a Gender Equality Scheme which would lay out how that authority will carry out their duties under this Order and Code of Practice.

O   Develop and publish a policy on equal pay arrangements.

O   Continuously assess the impact of new legislation, policies and changes in employment or service delivery issues.

Territorial Extent and Implementation

The Code of Practice, in respect of the general gender equality duty applies to England, Wales and any reserved public function in

Scotland. Otherwise, it is essentially applicable to England and to English agencies whose functions extend into devolved territories.

Whilst the Code or Practice applies to what are called "Public Authorities", its requirements can also be applied to any private/commercial organisation carrying out a public function. The CEHR states clearly that where a commercial or voluntary organisation is fulfilling, say, a contract for a public authority, it takes on the gender equality responsibilities of a public authority. The CEHR has a helpline for organisations requiring support with these responsibilities. Regional numbers are to be found on their website; the address is given below.

*"The duties of public authorities apply all along the public sector supply chain. They are also relevant to public/private partnerships and private finance initiatives."*
www.equalityhumanrights.com (the CEHR website, public authorities pages)

Enforcement and Sanctions

If a public authority fails to comply with its duties, the CEHR may issue a compliance notice against it. The offending authority must then meet its duty and report back to CEHR within 28 days. If the CEHR is not satisfied after three months, it can apply for a court order to ensure compliance.

Only the CEHR, rather than individuals, can apply to the court although a judicial review would be available where appropriate.

The CEHR has overall responsibility for monitoring the effectiveness and uptake of these new duties, publishing a review every three years. Obviously any relevant inspectorates would be expected to take compliance into account.

**Equal Pay Act 1970/1975**

This Act was passed in 1970 but did not come into force until 1975. Essentially, the Act states that men and women should receive equal pay for work of equal value.

## Race Relations Act 1976

The Race Relations Act is essentially modelled on the Sex Discrimination Act and even though the issues/problems covered are very different the approaches are very similar.

Once again, this Act uses the terms direct and indirect discrimination. It adds a third type of discrimination – victimisation.

Discrimination by means of victimisation means treating the person less favourably because that person has made a complaint or allegation of discrimination, or has acted as a witness or informant in connection with such an allegation, or intends to do so.

This Act makes discrimination on the grounds of race illegal. Race is defined in terms of colour, race, nationality or ethnic or national origins. It does not cover religion. However, a group of people that have established their own racial identity around their religion may be treated under the Act as a distinct ethnic group.   For example, Sikhs have been treated under the Act as a distinct ethnic group.
The areas covered by the Act are education, housing, employment, public and private clubs, entertainment and the provision of goods and services.

The Race Relations (Amendment) Act 2000 has strengthened the original 1976 Act.  Public bodies (e.g. local authorities) now have a general statutory duty to eliminate unlawful racial discrimination and to promote equality of opportunity and good relations between persons of different racial groups (s.71).

As a result of European Union Directive 2000/43/EC (Equal Treatment of People Irrespective of Racial or Ethnic Origin) the Race Relations 1976 (Amendment) Regulations 2003 have made various changes to the 1976 Act.  These include:

O   A new definition of harassment on the ground of a person's race, ethnic or national origins

O   It is unlawful for an employer to subject an employee or an applicant to racial harassment

O   It is unlawful for public bodies concerned with the provision of health, welfare or other services to subject persons to harassment

**O**    A re-definition, but continued recognition, that being of a particular race, ethnic or national origin can be a determining requirement for a particular employment

The 1976 Act set up the Commission for Racial Equality, which has now been replaced by the Commission for Equality and Human Rights.

Once again, this Act allows for positive action in order to encourage members of a particular group to participate if they have been under represented, or to ensure the welfare of a particular group.

## NHS and Community Care Act 1990

This piece of legislation is often referred to as the Community Care Act. However, it is actually the National Health Service and Community Care Act. We look at the Act in more detail in Section Nine.

This Act formalised the shift away from institutions and towards care in the community. It also separated purchasing of services and the provision of services - often referred to as the purchaser, provider split.

Although there is no specific part of the Act which refers to oppression/discrimination the clear ethos of the Act is about "needs led" assessment. This means an individual should be assessed by a care manager who will identify the needs of the individual and then ensure the purchasing of services to meet these needs. Clearly a needs led assessment should address issues of culture, sexuality etc. Specifically ignoring these needs would therefore be against the spirit of the Act.

## Disability Discrimination Act 1995

This Act establishes various legal rights for people with disabilities. It makes it unlawful to discriminate against people with disabilities in employment, access to goods, services, transport and education.

The Act defines a disabled person as someone who has:-

*"A physical or mental impairment which has a substantial and long term adverse effect on (their) ability to carry out normal day-to-day activities"*

This Act does state that in terms of people with a disability and employment some discrimination may be *"justifiable"*. The introduction of this concept of justification into direct discrimination in this Act is in marked contrast to both the Sex Discrimination Act and the Race Relations Act where direct discrimination is incapable of justification. This Act has recently been strengthened by the introduction of the Disability Discrimination Act 2005, (see below).

## Race Relations (Amendment) Act 2000

This Act strengthens the original Race Relations Act 1976 (all the sections of the 2000 Act are inserted into the original 1976 Act).

## Disability Discrimination Act 2005

This Act introduces new duties onto public authorities. These duties are that in carrying out their functions public authorities are to have due regard to:

O  The need to eliminate discrimination against people with disabilities that is unlawful

O  The need to eliminate harassment that is unlawful

O  The need to promote equality of opportunity between disabled persons and other persons

O  The need to take steps to take account of disabled person's disabilities, even where that involves treating disabled person's more favourably than other persons.

This Act still allows for situations where discrimination is justifiable, but the impression is this should be in exceptional circumstances only (eg. disproportionate costs involved). All the key sections of the 2005 Act are inserted into the DDA 1995.

## Sexual Orientation

The Employment Equality (Sexual Orientation) Regulations 2003 were introduced in response to EU Directive 2000/78/EC (establishing a general framework for equal treatment in employment). The 2003 Regulations make it unlawful to discriminate on the grounds of sexual orientation in the area of employment.

## Employment Equality in Respect of Religion and Belief

In respect of employment, recruitment and education discrimination (direct, indirect or harassment) against a person because of their religion or belief is unlawful under the Employment Equality (Religion or Belief) Regulations 2003. However there are exceptions allowed within these Regulations in situations where being of a particular religion or belief is a genuine and determining occupational requirement.

## Employment Equality in Respect of Age

Through the Employment Equality (Age) Regulations 2006, people cannot be discriminated in work or training on the basis of age. If an employer does introduce an age related condition, there must be an objective work related justification for this. An employer can require staff to retire at the age of 65 but must give them six months notice. The employee has the right to request to continue working. The employer can still decide to retire the employee.

## Equality Act 2006

Each of the main anti-discriminatory Acts, Sex Discrimination Act 1975, Race Relations Act 1976 and Disability Discrimination Act 1995 established their own Commission. However, the equality agenda has widened. Through the European Union new regulations have made the discrimination of people on the grounds of sexual orientation, religion or belief and age unlawful. These new regulations apply to work and training only. Additionally there was no organisation responsible for promoting equality in these new areas. The Government therefore decided to establish a commission responsible for promoting equal opportunities for all. Additionally, although public bodies have to adhere to the Human Rights Act 1998 no public body exists to promote the Human Rights Act. This duty has also been given to the new Commission.

## Commission for Equality and Human Rights (CEHR)

This Commission is established by s.1 of the 2006 Act. The CEHR has a general duty (s.3) to encourage and support the development of a society in which:

a)  people's ability to achieve their potential is not limited by prejudice or discrimination

b)  there is respect for and protection of each individual's human rights

c)  there is respect for the dignity and worth of each individual

d)  each individual has an equal opportunity to participate in society

e)  there is mutual respect between groups based on understanding and valuing of diversity and on shared respect for equality and human rights.

The CEHR is to pursue these objectives by:

O   Promoting equality of opportunity and diversity

O   Enforcing anti-discriminatory legislation

O   Promote awareness, understanding and protection of human rights.

The CEHR has the power to:

O   Issue codes of practice to assist organisations to comply with legislation

O   Initiate enquiries and investigations

O   Issue notices requiring people to comply with anti-discriminatory legislation

O   Assist individuals take legal proceedings where anti-discriminatory legislation appears to have been violated

The Equality Act 2006 also makes additional forms of discrimination unlawful. These being:

O   Direct or indirect discrimination against people on the basis of their religion or beliefs (this includes a person who has no beliefs). Areas covered include the provision of goods, facilities, services or property. There are a range of exceptions. Religious organisations can make adhering to their religion a requirement for membership. Religious charities can provide benefits only to people of a specific religion.

O  The Secretary of State is given the power to make regulations which will make discrimination, on the grounds of sexual orientations, unlawful.

O  An additional duty on public authorities is inserted into the SDA 1975 (to promote equality of opportunity between men and women).

The previous Commissions:

O  Equal Opportunities Commission

O  Commission for Racial Equality

O  Disability Rights Commission

have now been replaced by the Commission for Equality and Human Rights.

 ### In Summary

It is important to know about the major pieces of social legislation affecting your practice in this area. However, the law is very limited in scope and best practice is way ahead of legislation.

# ( 5 ) RIGHTS

Within English and Welsh law it has traditionally been the case that laws that are introduced by Parliament state what actions or behaviours constitute an offence. In other words the law tells us what we cannot do. The implication of this is that so long as we do not do something that is an offence the action is lawful or we have a right to do it. However, this is only by implication and in effect different people have been treated differently (discriminated against) in all sorts of ways in Britain.

In the period from 1970 to the 1990's because of the grey areas in English and Welsh law many people who felt their rights had not been upheld in English law took their cases to the European Court of Human Rights. This Court enforces the European Convention on Human Rights across all the European Countries that have signed the Convention. Britain is one of these countries. The European Convention states rights positively. It makes clear what our rights are. If we are stopped from exercising one of these rights we can take our claim to the European Court.

The European Convention on Human Rights and the work of the Court were so successful that Parliament decided to make the European Convention part of English and Welsh law.

This chapter will cover:

- Human Rights Act 1998
- Police and Criminal Evidence Act 1984
- National Health Service and Community Care Act 1990
- Carers (Recognition and Services) Act 1995
- Carers and Disabled Children Act 2000
- The Right to Direct Payments
- Carers (Equal Opportunities) Act 2004
- Civil Partnership Act 2004

## Human Rights Act 1998

The Human Rights Act 1998 was introduced by Parliament and came into force in October 2000. It is, in effect, the European Convention on Human Rights.

Listed in Schedule 1 of the Act are various rights. These include:

*Article 2*

Everyone's right to life shall be protected by law.

*Article 3*

No one shall be subjected to……….degrading……..treatment.

*Article 5*

Everyone has the right to liberty and security of person.

*Article 8*

Everyone has the right to respect for his private and family life and his correspondence.

*Article 9*

Everyone has the right to freedom of thought, conscience and religion.

*Article 12*

Men and women of marriageable age have the right to marry and to found a family.

*Article 14*

The enjoyment of these rights and freedoms set forth in this Convention shall be secured without discrimination on any ground….

Implications of the Human Rights Act 1998

It is still not clear what the impact of this Act will be. It will only be as a result of cases brought before courts in England and Wales that its full implications will be known.

However, there are presently various practices in services that <u>may</u> infringe one or other of the rights listed in the Act. Courts will only make a judgement if an individual, possibly supported by an organisation, takes a claim of infringed or violated rights to the court.

Practices that services should review include the following:-

1. In various residential services the main doors are locked by staff. This is often for good and understandable reasons e.g. reduce the likelihood of intruders entering the building or others who should not be there.

   In nearly all residential homes whenever someone wants to leave and they cannot operate the lock (for whatever reason) a staff member will assist them. However some services use locked front doors more as a means of keeping people in rather than keeping intruders out. Services must be clear why they lock their front door and what they do if someone who wants to leave but cannot operate the lock (and may need support outside) tries to open the door.

   If a service locks a front door knowing that some individuals want to leave but cannot operate the lock (or do not have a key) then it could amount to infringing the person's right to liberty.

   Some advice and guidance is contained in the Mental Health Act 1983 Code of Practice.

2. Within services there are individuals who have behaviour which challenges. Some people who have behaviour which challenges are placed in services alongside vulnerable people. Sometimes the vulnerable individuals can be subject to assault from the person with behaviour which challenges. This assault may be hair pulling, pushing over, kicking or hitting.

If it becomes clear that vulnerable individuals are at risk from the individuals with behaviours which challenge then the service should act to protect the vulnerable individuals. If the vulnerable individual is subject to further assault then a complaint could be made to a court. If it could be argued that the individual's right to be free from degrading treatment (article 3) had been infringed by the service in not acting comprehensively enough to protect the vulnerable person then the complaint may be upheld. Even if such a scenario does not represent a violation of an individuals rights to be free from degrading treatment services should carefully consider whether vulnerable people should be in the same service as individuals with behaviour which challenges.

These are just two examples but there will probably be many other examples that could arise from the implementation of the Human Rights Act 1998. Services and staff should welcome this Act. It will hopefully lead to raised standards and expectations which will be for the benefit of all.

Other pieces of legislation do positively state a limited number of rights. Whilst we have given brief details here of what rights are contained in the legislation see Section Nine for more details on the specific Acts.

### Police and Criminal Evidence Act 1984

o    establishes the rights of all people arrested by the police

o    detainees have the right to legal advice (on request) and the right to have the police notify a person who is likely to have an interest in their welfare

o    the Act and associated Code of Practice also refers to the involvement of "appropriate adults" (see page 104-105)

### National Health Service and Community Care Act 1990

o    individuals with social care needs have the right to an assessment of their needs

o    individuals have the right to complain

o    this Act also attempted to introduce the right of a person to choose which service if the assessment had identified that the person needed a service

### Carers (Recognition and Services) Act 1995

This applies to all people who act as a principal carer for another person. The Act gives carer's the right to an assessment of their own needs when the person they are caring for is having their needs assessed by social services.

## Carers and Disabled Children Act 2000

This Act extends the right of carers to an assessment of their own needs. A carer can request an assessment of their needs at any time if they provide a substantial amount of care. Social services has a duty to respond to such a request. Following the assessment of the carers needs, social services has the power to supply certain services to the carer.

The Carers (Equal Opportunities) Act 2004 amends the Carers and Disabled Children Act 2000. The 2004 Act inserts two duties:

O   Local authorities, when they are in contact with carers or service users, are to inform carers who may be eligible for an assessment of their right to a carers assessment.

O   When conducting a carers assessment consideration must be given to the carers work, education, training or leisure activities (or their wish to undertake such work or other activities).

Additionally the 2000 Act empowers social services to make direct payments to carers (instead of arranging a service). The carer then uses the money to arrange services themselves to meet their own assessed needs.

The 2000 Act also gives social services the power to charge carers for services they receive.

## Carers (Equal Opportunities) Act 2004

This Act covers both England and Wales.

The Act gives carers new rights to information about assessment. It amends previous carers legislation to state that local authorities have a duty to inform carers of their right to an assessment.

Section 2 of the Act states that a carer's assessment must take into account whether the carer works or wants to work, any courses the carer is taking or wants to take and any other leisure activities the carer undertakes or wants to undertake.

The Act also encourages authorities to work in co-operation by giving local authorities new powers to enlist the help of housing, health, education and other local authorities to provide support to carers. If the local authority makes a request to another authority to plan services, that authority must give the request due consideration.

## The Right to Direct Payments

Direct Payments have evolved since first introduced through the Community Care (Direct Payments) Act 1996. As a result of s.57 of the Health and Social Care Act 2001 the Secretary of State can make regulations requiring local authorities to offer direct payments to an adult who is eligible for social care services. These Regulations were introduced in 2003. In effect an adult who meets the requirements has a right to a direct payment.

The White Paper, Our Health, Our Care, Our Say (Department of Health 2006) made clear the Government's intentions to extend the take up of direct payments. The Government will introduce legislation to enable an agent, acting on behalf of a person who lacks capacity, to request direct payments for the person who lacks capacity.

## Civil Partnership Act 2004

This Act establishes the right of same sex couples to enter into a civil partnership. This is not a marriage but is a relationship of equivalent seriousness and commitment. The registration of the civil partnership is in a procedure similar to a civil marriage.

Two individuals can enter into a civil partnership if:

O   they are of the same sex
O   neither is in an existing civil partnership nor presently married
O   they are not related to each other in a manner that would bar them from entering into a civil partnership
O   they are both 16 or over

Individuals aged 16 or 17 need their parents permission to enter into a civil partnership. The 2004 Act outlines related responsibilities and rights of a civil partnership eg. occupancy rights etc.

## In Summary

Previously, issues of rights have not had a high profile within the English and Welsh legislative framework. However, the implementation of the Human Rights Act 1998 will have a major impact, bringing England and Wales into line with many of its European counterparts. The true impact that the Act will have within social care services is yet to be seen. However, we anticipate that many current practices may well infringe some of the rights listed within the Act.

# 6    CONFIDENTIALITY

Confidentiality is a major issue within health and social care and this is quite rightly reflected within the NVQ framework. There are a number of pieces of legislation which pertain to confidentiality and social care. This chapter will cover:

O   Access to Medical Reports Act 1988
O   Data Protection Act 1998
O   Freedom of Information Act 2000

## Data Protection Act 1998

This Act came into force on 1 March 2000. It replaced all of the Data Protection Act 1984 and the Access to Personal Files Act 1987. It also replaced most of the Access to Health Records Act 1990.

Individuals have a right of access to information about them held by social services departments, housing organisations or health professionals.

An individual has a right of access to all information held about them. Adults with a learning disability or a mental health problem have a right to see their file if they understand the nature of the request. Children can request to see their file and it has to be complied with if they understand the nature of the request.

Social services or health professionals can refuse access to all or part of a person's file for certain reason e.g. where access to the information would be likely to cause serious harm to the physical or mental health of the data subject or another person. Withholding of information is expected to be used in exceptional circumstances only.

If a person is refused access to information they can appeal to either the courts or the Information Commissioner (formerly called the Data Protection Commissioner).

O   The courts can order disclosure

O   The Information Commissioner can issue an enforcement notice (effectively enforce disclosure).

Where a person has seen their file and feels that information is inaccurate in any way they may request the file to be amended. If they feel that social services has not done this they can go to the Information Commissioner or the courts to enforce correction of inaccurate information.

This Act also provides individuals with a right of access to personal information that relates to them that is held by commercial organisations on computer (e.g. insurance companies, etc).

There are several enforceable principles that underpin the DPA. These principles include:-

O    information about a person must be obtained lawfully and fairly

O    the information must only be used for the specified purpose

O    information must be relevant, adequate and not excessive

O    information must be accurate and kept up-to-date

O    information must be kept no longer than necessary for the purposes specified

O    organisations must have in place measures to ensure personal information is not unlawfully processed, lost or destroyed

Social care staff have to balance the requirement to uphold confidentiality with the need to share relevant information with staff and professionals who work with a particular service user. When the service user first had their assessment it should have been made clear to them that other professionals would need to know information about them. This should also have been conveyed to the service user when they started receiving a service. Potentially quite a lot of people will need to know a fair amount of information about a particular person. However staff should only know information if it, in some way, enhances the quality of care the service user experiences.

## Access to Medical Reports Act 1988

This Act gives individuals the right to see a medical report that is written by a doctor for employment or insurance purposes.  The individual can comment on the report or ask for changes if they feel it is inaccurate.

## Freedom of Information Act 2000

Direct care staff, support workers and professionals in regular contact with service users and family members should not get confused by the recent implementation of this Act.

The Freedom of Information Act 2000 gives ordinary people the right to request information from public authorities (local authorities, police, NHS organisations) about statistics and about decision making and policy making.

Information about specific individuals, such as service users or patients, remains confidential and can only be accessed by the service user themselves in line with the Data Protection Act 1998.

## In Summary

It is important to be aware of the legislation which is relevant in this area, not only to ensure that you are acting within the law but also to help you to advise people on their rights in terms of access to files.

Access to files is also a spur to good practice. Anything recorded should be relevant, factual and balanced. The person you are writing about may read their file next week.

# (7) HEALTH AND SAFETY

Issues of health and safety are vital in every work role. In terms of legislation, health and safety is generally covered by statutory regulations. Perhaps this is because regulations are more easily changed than Acts of Parliament and health and safety issues need to be kept under constant review.

This chapter will cover:

- Health and Safety at Work Act 1974
- Food Safety Act 1990
- Environmental Protection Act 1990
- Corporate Manslaughter and Corporate Homicide Act 2007

and associated regulations

## Health and Safety at Work Act 1974

This Act outlines a number of responsibilities for employers, managers and employees.

*Employers* have a duty to:-

O   ensure the health and safety at work for all employees

O   provide and maintain equipment and systems which are safe and not a risk to employees' health in terms of use, handling, storage and transport of articles and substances

O   provide information, training and supervision relating to health and safety at work

*Managers* have a duty to:-

O   maintain a safe working environment for all staff

O   ensure that all staff adhere to policies, procedures and instructions

O   provide training for staff practices and work methods

O   explain hazards and safe working practices to new employees before they start work

O   report/record all accidents

*Employees* have a duty to:-

O   adhere to instructions relating to the operation of a site and equipment

O   ensure that they use materials in line with recommended procedures

O   utilise protective clothing and equipment as directed

O   not to misuse anything provided for health, safety and welfare

Associated Regulations

There are a range of regulations in the health and safety area.  To aid compliance, the health and Safety Executive (HSE) implement new regulations on only two dates per year.  These are:

- 6<sup>th</sup> April
- 1<sup>st</sup> October

It is hoped that this will enable organizations to foresee change and plan for it.

The HSE publish an excellent (and brief) overview of current legislation – Health and Safety Regulation: a short guide. This can be downloaded from the HSE website at www.hse.gov.uk.

**Safety Representatives and Safety Committees Regulations**

If an employer recognises a trade union and that union has either appointed or is about to appoint safety representatives then the employer must consult those representatives on matters which will affect the employees they represent.

The roles of trade union safety representatives appointed under these Regulations are:-

- to investigate possible dangers at work, the causes of accidents and general complaints by employees on health and safety and welfare issues and to take these matters up with the employer
- to carry out inspections of the workplace particularly following accidents, diseases or other events
- to represent employees in discussions with health and safety inspectors and to receive information from those inspectors
- to attend meetings of safety committees

An employer must set up a safety committee if two or more trade union representatives ask for one.

**Health and Safety (First Aid) Regulations**

These Regulations require employers to provide adequate equipment, facilities and personnel to enable first aid to be given to employees if they become ill or are injured at work.

The Regulations do not oblige employers to provide first aid for members of the public, though the Health and Safety Executive strongly recommends that employers make provision for them.

## Workplace (Health, Safety and Welfare) Regulations

These Regulations complement the Management of Health and Safety at Work Regulations, and cover the management of workplaces. Duties are placed on both employers and employees (in the sense that both have control over a workplace). The main requirements created by these Regulations are:-

o  the workplace, equipment, systems etc must be maintained in an efficient state

o  enclosed workplaces must be ventilated by a sufficient quantity of fresh and purified air

o  a reasonable temperature must be maintained inside buildings and a sufficient number of thermometers must be provided

o  lighting must be suitable and efficient

o  workplaces must be kept sufficiently clean

## Manual Handling Operations Regulations

These cover what is often referred to as "moving and handling". The Regulations contain the following main requirements:-

o  suitable and efficient assessment of all moving and handling should be made, if the handling cannot be avoided

o  risk reduction strategies must be considered by employers to reduce the risk of injury to the lowest level reasonably practicable

o  employers must provide reasonable information about moving and handling

o  employers must review assessments where there is reason to suspect that circumstances have changed, and then make any necessary changes

o  employees must make full and proper use of any system of work provided by the employer

## Reporting of Injuries, Diseases and Dangerous Occurrences Regulations

These Regulations are often referred to as RIDDOR. The Regulations require the reporting of work-related accidents, diseases and dangerous occurrences. Employers, self employed people and people in control of work premises have duties under the Regulations to report:

O   deaths or major injuries at work

O   work related injuries which result in people being away from work for over 3 days

O   work related diseases

O   dangerous occurrences at work

## Health and Safety (Consultation with Employees) Regulations

Any employees not in groups covered by trade union safety representatives must be consulted by their employers under these Regulations. An employer can choose to consult them directly or through elected representatives.

Elected representatives of employees have the following roles:-

O   to take up with employers concerns about possible risks and dangerous events in the workplace that may affect the employees they represent

O   to take up with employers general matters affecting the health and safety of the employees they represent

O   to represent the employees who elected them in consultations with Health and Safety inspectors

Employers may choose to give elected representatives extra roles.

## Management of Health and Safety at Work Regulations

These Regulations place on employers a duty to assess all health and safety risks associated with their work and to introduce procedures and practices that minimise the likelihood of any identified risks occurring.

Additionally employers have to provide training for staff:-

O when they start work

O when their work or responsibilities change and there are new or greater risks

O periodically if needed - for instance if the skills do not get used regularly

The training must be during working hours and not at the expense of employees.

## Control of Substances Hazardous to Health Regulations

These Regulations are often referred to as COSHH.

The Regulations cover substances which can cause ill health. Any substances such as cleaning materials, waste products, fumes etc are covered.

In order to comply with the Regulations employers must:-

O assess the risks to health arising from work

O decide what precautions are needed

O prevent or control exposure to substances hazardous to health

O ensure that control measures are used and maintained

O monitor exposure of workers to hazardous substances and where assessment shows that health surveillance may be needed to carry out such surveillance

O ensure that employees are properly informed, trained and supervised.

## Product Liability

Product liability is established under Part 1 of the Consumer Protection Act 1987. Product liability means that under the Consumer

Protection Act 1987 a manufacturer is liable for injury caused, or property that is damaged, due to faulty equipment that they have provided. The manufacturer is also responsible for providing information about the safe use of the equipment. Hence instructions are often stuck to equipment as well as being provided in leaflets or booklets. Product liability could apply equally to hoists, other aids and adaptations as well as an office chair.

If the equipment is not faulty and is used satisfactorily then liability for its safe use transfers to the employer.

## Provision and Use of Equipment Regulations (PUWER)

These Regulations impose a range of duties on employers (and to a limited extent to the employees who use the equipment). Aspects include:

O The initial state of the equipment

O Use of equipment for the proper purpose

O Suitability of equipment

O Maintenance

O Inspection

O Training staff in it's use

The scope of these Regulations has been interpreted very broadly so that it includes cupboards and curtain rails as well as equipment that is subject to heavy usage. The employer's liability is strictly applied. Even if the equipment was regularly inspected and then it unexpectedly fell and injured a staff member the employer is still liable. The employer would not be liable for negligence if the equipment was satisfactorily maintained and inspected, but they would still be liable for any injury under these Regulations.

## Lifting Operations and Lifting Equipment Regulations

These Regulations apply to lifting equipment used at work. Lifting equipment would include hoists, stairlifts and through floor lifts. The Regulations impose a range of duties on employers and to a limited extent on staff who use or supervise the use of the equipment. Duties include:

O   Ensuring adequate strength and stability

O   Positioning and installation

O   Marking of safe working loads

O   Organisation of lifting operations

O   Examination and inspection

O   Reporting defects, and acting on these reports

There is no set guidance as to how frequently lifting equipment should be inspected. This is partly dependent on whether the equipment is exposed to conditions that could cause it to deteriorate such that dangerous situations could arise. Some hoist manufacturers recommend a thorough examination of their hoists every six months. Against this the Health and Safety Executive have published a document recommending that hoists are inspected at least every twelve months. The implication is that some manufacturers could have a conflict of interests. (That is they can charge a care organisation every time their trained inspectors go out on a visit.) What is clear is that the time scales for thorough inspections should be drawn up by a competent person who is aware of all relevant facts.

**Food Safety Act 1990**

This Act applies wherever food is supplied other than within a family situation. Therefore, all social care settings which involve the supply of food must comply with hygiene and other food safety requirements.

This Act is a wide ranging piece of legislation which strengthened and updated existing laws relevant to food safety. The Act sets out a number of requirements about food produced for human consumption:-

O   food provided must not be injurious to health

O   it must not be unfit to eat

O   it must not be contaminated

The Food Safety Act and all food legislation is enforced through environmental health officers and trading standards officers who are employed by local authorities.

## Food Hygiene (England) Regulations

These new food hygiene regulations came into force in 2006 and bring together recent European legislation and update the Food Safety Act 1990.

They are said to present a new "flexible" approach to food hygiene practice whilst optimising public health and setting in place new responsibilities and penalties. Of the many requirements it contains, one stands out in the context of this book:

*"All operators of food businesses must register with their Local Authority Environmental Health Department and that includes kitchens of care establishments and public sector organisations."*

The kitchen manager is responsible for responding to these regulations and ensuring staff are aware of them too. The HSE document "Food Law Code of Practice" makes specific mention of the need to particularly safeguard people who are deemed vulnerable from poor hygiene practice. For such critical legislation, it is important to get the whole story. The Food Law Code of Practice document entitled "Safer Food, Better Business" can be obtained free from the HSE or by telephoning: 0845 606 0667.

## Environmental Protection Act 1990

This is a very wide ranging piece of legislation, much of which is probably not relevant to social care staff. Some sections, however, may have a direct bearing on your work. For example, section 34 of the Act places a duty of care on anyone who *"produces, imports, carries, keeps, treats or disposes of household, commercial, or industrial "* waste.

In addition, the Environmental Protection Act contains the main legislation for England and Wales on statutory nuisance. A variety of definitions of statutory nuisance are outlined within the Act. However, those which may be most relevant to care staff are:-

O    any premises in such a state as to be prejudicial to health or a nuisance.

O    noise emitted from premises so as to be prejudicial to health or a nuisance.

## Regulatory Reform (Fire Safety) Order 2005

This Statutory Instrument reforms the fire safety regulations that apply to England and Wales.

In any workplace the employer has a responsibility to:

O    take fire precautions to ensure, as far as possible, the safety of all employees

O    to ensure there are general fire precautions to keep the property safe (and so protect the general public) (article 8)

The employers duties include:

O    carry out a risk assessment to identify the general fire precautions that are needed and then (article 9)

O    apply any fire prevention measure and have in place an evacuation procedure (articles 10 to 18)

O    inform employees of the risks and the fire prevention measures (articles 19 to 21)

Employees have duties which include (article 23)

O    follow all fire safety requirements as directed by their employer

O    inform the employer of any risks not adequately addressed

## Corporate Manslaughter and Corporate Homicide Act 2007

This Act received Royal Assent on 26th July 2007. It amends case law and generally the Law of Negligence

Most of this Act came into force on 6th April 2008 and it basically does just one thing; it creates a new offence of Corporate Manslaughter, or in Scotland, Corporate Homicide. The differing terminology is simply in order to fit with existing legal structures on each side of the border. The Act is, aside from this, UK wide legislation.

The offence of Corporate Manslaughter/Homicide is not new however, but has always been wrapped up in a mass of case law and other legislation known collectively as the Law of Negligence. In the old system, a company could only be convicted if one high up individual, known legally as a "controlling mind" could be seen as almost personally culpable for the death of a person through the company's activities. Years of accident investigations have shown that fatal incidents, and indeed corporations, do not work like that. There is usually a string of events that lead to an incident.

The new Act therefore redefines the offence and the causes required to be present for a case of Corporate manslaughter to be brought. It happens like this:

O A death occurs. Obvious really, but if someone is "only" severely injured, standard health and safety legislation still applies.

O The death does not have to be an employee of the company concerned but it does have to result from the way that company's activities were managed or organised.

O Also, the death must have arisen from a gross breach of the company's duty of care to the victim.

O Lastly, the organisational failings that led to the death must have been somehow authorised by senior management. That is to say, practices that were authored, or agreed to, or known about by senior management. Senior management does not just include Directors either.

Please also note that this Act does not introduce any new duties on organisations but does, interestingly, extend to organisations engaged in illegal activities. The Act applies to any business in the UK or foreign businesses operating in the UK from partnerships upwards. Single traders are not covered. Crown Bodies and government organisations are covered including the Prison Service and the Army.

In order that certain people doing dangerous jobs can get on and do them without their employers being paralysed by legislation there are certain exemptions, where charges under this Act may not be brought. Some are "comprehensive", for example soldiers in battle and training, while others are "partial" which is where some aspects of social care come in.

<u>Partial Exemptions</u>

While social work and probation departments are still covered by this Act in their duties as employers and occupiers of buildings; they are exempt from prosecution under this Act when their staff are carrying out statutory inspection functions and other frontline aspects of their jobs. It is difficult to see how this will work in practice and it will be shaped by case law but if, for example, a social worker visits a house to investigate a claim of abuse and is killed by a client then, provided their employer had not failed in their duties as an employer, no charge can be brought against the employer under this Act. Other occupations subject to partial exemptions include lifeboat crews and mountain rescue teams which rather puts the job into perspective doesn't it?

 **In Summary**

We all have responsibilities in terms of health and safety at work. It is important to be aware of these responsibilities and to have at least a basic understanding of the law which informs this area of practice.

# ( 8 ) SEXUALITY ISSUES

Staff working within social care can come across a variety of issues to do with sexuality. Often, as individuals, we remain ignorant of much of the legislation relating to this area as it is not often discussed.

Considerations of sexuality and the law can arise within services for people with a learning disability and to a lesser extent in other services where an adult may be vulnerable due to mental health problems.

This section will discuss issues of sexuality positively. Chapter Nine addresses options for protecting vulnerable people from abuse.

It is the intention of the law to protect vulnerable people from abuse and exploitation. It is not the intention of the law to prohibit consensual sexual relationships between people who understand what they are engaging in. The Guidance to the Sexual Offences Act 2003 (Home Office 2004:28) makes this explicit by saying:

> "..... it is important to appreciate that where a person with a mental disorder is able to consent freely to sexual activity they have the same rights to engage in consensual sexual activity as anyone else"

---

## The Sexual Offences Act 2003

This Act was implemented in May 2004. It seeks to rationalise and modernise the legislation relating to sexual offences that was scattered across several sexual offences acts dating from 1956 to 2000.

### Consent

Consent is defined in s.74 of the 2003 Act. A person consents if they agree by choice and they have the freedom and capacity to make that choice. The capacity to make the choice applies to that specific act (whatever that act is). It is not a blanket capacity test. In other words a person may not have the capacity to agree to a financial contract, but they may have the capacity to agree to engage in a sexual activity with another person.

Whether certain sexual acts are offences, or not, will hinge on the issue of consent. The Sexual Offences Act 2003 establishes three main situations that would result in sexual activity with a person with a learning disability or a mental health problem being viewed as non-consensual. They are:

1.  The nature of the person's learning disability or mental health problem means they lack the capacity to make choices about specific sexual activities (as written below in section on labelling and classification).

2.  Due to having a learning disability or mental health problem the person is vulnerable to inducements, threats or deception.

3.  The person with a learning disability or mental health problem is in a relationship of care. Even if the person with a learning disability or mental health problem consented to sex with a care worker or professional this consent cannot be viewed as freely given.

## Labelling and Classification

The term used in the 2003 Act is "mental disorder". The definition of mental disorder was drawn from section 1 of the Mental Health Act 1983. This definition has since been amended by the Mental Health Act 2007 to "any disorder or disability of the mind." (see pages 93-95)

The definition includes all people with a learning disability and all people with a mental health problem.

Additionally some sections of the 2003 Act relate to protecting people who have *"a mental disorder impeding choice"* (lack capacity to consent to sexual activities).

The 2003 Act defines the lack of capacity to consent to sexual activity as:

O    The person lacks sufficient understanding of the nature or reasonably foreseeable consequences of the sexual act.

O    The person is unable to communicate a choice

O    Or for any other reason lacks the capacity to choose

The guidance that supports the Act suggests that sufficient understanding of the nature of the Act might include knowing that sexual activity is different from personal care. (If this threshold is used in court it means it is a very low threshold. We will only know if this particular interpretation is used as a result of cases going to court under this new Act.) Reasonably foreseeable consequences might include the knowledge that some sexual activities can lead to pregnancy or the transmission of disease.

Other reasons why a person may be unable to refuse might include not understanding that they had a choice (due to institutionalisation) or because they have a condition that might affect their ability to make a choice.

There is a degree of subtlety in the way the term 'mental disorder impeding choice' is defined. It is not intended to be a blanket term. Therefore a person may have the label severe learning disability but if they have the capacity to agree to a sexual activity then they can engage in that activity with a consensual partner. Additionally if a person with a mild learning disability can not comprehend what is involved in a sexual activity then arguably they do not have the capacity to consent to that activity.

If services want people with a learning disability to enjoy an ordinary life then it means services have a responsibility to ensure that the opportunities for service users to make decisions are maximized. In terms of sexual relationships this means that services need to support service users acquire knowledge about sexual relationships. Acquiring this knowledge could mean the difference between having the capacity to choose or lacking the capacity to decide.

In coming to a decision as to whether a person has the capacity to make a choice about engaging in sexual activity professionals must act in a responsible manner and be able to explain why they have made their decision. Carson (1989) points out that if service users are labelled by professionals then this could result in opportunities being restricted or limited.

If such labeling is not justified then the professionals would be vulnerable to a complaint being made against them.

### General Law

Sixteen year old women and men may enter into sexual relations with members of the opposite sex.

Women may enter into homosexual relationships at 16. Men may enter into homosexual relationships at 16.

Sixteen year old women and men may marry with parental consent. A couple may marry without parental consent at the age of 18.

### Marriage

Anybody aged 18 or over may marry. The officiant (Registrar or Religious Minister) must be satisfied that the individuals understand the nature of the proposed undertaking. It has been judicially stated that "the contract of marriage is in its essence one of simplicity" and therefore understandable by most people. If the officiant has any doubts about such capacity to marry s/he may ask a professional person to provide a statement.

## Civil Partnerships

The Civil Partnerships Act 2004 establishes the right of same sex couples to enter into a civil partnership. This is not marriage but is a relationship of equivalent seriousness and commitment. The registration of the civil partnership will be in a procedure similar to a civil marriage.

Two individuals can enter into a civil partnership if:

O   they are of the same sex
O   neither is in a existing civil partnership or presently married
O   they are not related to each other in a forbidden degree
O   they are both 16 or over

Within the 2004 Act related responsibilities and rights are listed in respect of occupancy rights, etc.

## The Human Rights Act 1998

The Human Rights Act 1998 has two articles that are particularly relevant to issues of sexuality. These being:

Article 8:   Everyone has the right to respect for his private and family life, his home and his correspondence.

Article 12:   Men and women of marriageable age have the right to marry and to found a family, according to the national laws governing the exercise of this right.

## Practice Implications

O   A person with the label severe learning disability could consent to sex if they had sufficient understanding of the sexual activity they were going to engage in and they could freely make the choice (the person with the learning disability was not subjected to threats, deception or inducements). The provision of sex education by services could enable more people labelled as having a severe learning disability to have the capacity to choose.

O   A person who has a learning disability or a mental health problem and has the capacity to make choices about sexual activities can engage in sexual activities with a partner so long as there are no threats, inducements or deception involved. Hence, this could mean that a person with a learning disability could have a sexual relationship with a person who does not have a learning disability.

O   Where two people are wanting to get married and one or both have a learning disability the service can ensure they understand what is involved by providing a sex education programme to the individual or couple. By informing an officiant or minister of religion of this it could address any concerns they may feel about supporting the couple marry.

**In Summary**

Issues of sexuality are particularly sensitive and many people remain ignorant of legislation in this area. Staff often have a number of fears relating to supporting people in intimate relationships and may ask "Is it legal?" It is important that individual members of staff do not make decisions by themselves but consult with other professionals.

## 9 ) PROTECTING ADULTS FROM ABUSE

In work with children there is a clear legislative framework to child protection. However, in working with adults the law is not so straightforward. In this chapter we look at policy and legislation that is relevant to protecting adults from abuse. The legislation which may be relevant to you will depend upon your working environment and the form of abuse you are concerned about. After discussing generic initiatives aimed at protecting adults we then go onto cover legal options in terms of protecting people from financial abuse; sexual abuse, domestic violence and forced marriage. Once again, remember that this is a quick reference guide to a complex area - if you require more information you are advised to look at the relevant policy statements and laws. If you are in a situation where you have concerns of abuse, always consult with your line manager.

This Chapter will cover:

O  Safeguarding Vulnerable Groups Act 2006
O  No Secrets: Guidance on developing and implementing multi-agency policies and procedures to protect vulnerable adults from abuse (2000)
O  Care Standards Act 2000
O  Mental Capacity Act 2005
O  Family Law Act 1996
O  Protection from Harassment Act 1997
O  Housing Act 1996
O  Forced Marriage (Civil Protection) Act 2007

## Safeguarding Vulnerable Groups Act 2006

This Act received Royal Assent on 8th November 2006. This Act amends the Children Act 1989, the Teaching and Higher Education Act 1998, the Protection of Children Act 1999, the Care Standards Act 2000, the Childcare Act 2006, the Data Protection Act 1998 and the Adoption and Children Act 2002, among others.

In essence this Act is a major revision, and streamlining of the system for vetting people who work with children and vulnerable adults. It resulted from the Bichard Inquiry Report, published in June 2004. The previous system had been fragmented and only truly accurate on the date checks were first carried out. One aim of the new scheme is to make it proactive rather than reactive. The Act, and therefore the new scheme, applies across England and Wales with the scheme having close ties with Scotland.

The Act provides a legislative framework for a new vetting and barring scheme for people working with children or vulnerable adults. It classifies various paid and unpaid activities covered by the scheme and institutes a barring system to stop undesirable individuals from working in these occupations.

The Act sets up the Independent Barring Board (IBB) which maintains two lists; one for work with children and one for work with adults. The IBB also makes decisions about who goes on these lists. Under the scheme, there are four routes to inclusion on either or both lists:

O Automatic inclusion for receiving a caution or conviction for certain specified offences or other criteria such as inclusion on a foreign list with no right of appeal.

O Automatic inclusion for receiving a caution or conviction for certain specified offences but with the right of appeal.

O Specified Behaviours, called "relevant conduct" in the Act, which includes conduct which harms a child or vulnerable adult or conduct involving, for example, child pornography.

O Risk of Harm – this is where evidence suggests that an individual may present a risk of harm to children or vulnerable adults.

These last two do not lead to automatic inclusion but are subject to consideration by the IBB for inclusion on the appropriate list. It should be noted that these last two do not require a conviction. This blocks a loophole in the system where, for example, a community "knows" that a person presents a risk and police have genuine concerns but a conviction has not been possible. People included on these lists may not engage in "regulated" or "controlled" activities involving children or vulnerable adults and the Act creates various requirements and offences to ensure that they do not.

**No Secrets: Guidance on developing and implementing multi-agency policies and procedures to protect vulnerable adults from abuse (2000)**

This is guidance issued by the Department of Health in 2000; as such it does not have the full force of statute law. It is important for all social care staff to be aware that the Government wants all agencies to take seriously and to respond as fully as possible to situations where vulnerable adults are being abused.

In No Secrets the Department of Health makes clear its expectations for individual providers of care to minimise the risk of abuse by:

O   rigorous recruitment practices

O   take up of written references

O   all volunteers should be subject to the same checks as paid staff

Provider services are also to have in place guidelines detailing staff responsibilities and how they should respond to concerns about any abuse of a vulnerable adult. These guidelines are to link into, and be consistent with, the local multi-agency policy (bringing together social services, police, health services and provider services).

Provider services are also expected to ensure that service users, carers and the general public have accessible information detailing what abuse is, how they can raise concerns and/or make a complaint.

## Care Standards Act 2000

The Government introduced several measures intended to enhance the protection of vulnerable adults through the establishment of various organisations or initiatives. These were:

o establish a new more effective inspection service. This became the Commission for Social Care Inspection in 2004

o establish the General Social Care Council to facilitate the development of values and the registration of social care staff

o establish the Protection of Vulnerable Adults List (POVA). Any staff member who could have been or was successfully disciplined and sacked for putting a vulnerable adult at risk must have their name put on this list.

## Mental Capacity Act 2005

### Introduction

Although the Mental Capacity Act 2005 is discussed in the section Protecting Adults From Abuse, the intention of the 2005 Act is to promote good practice on a day to day basis when working with a woman or man who may lack capacity to make decisions.

### The Principles

Key principles are stated in s.1:

o a person is assumed to have capacity unless it is established that they lack capacity

o All practical steps to help a person make decisions must have been undertaken (without success) before treating them as unable to make a decision

o A person is not to be treated as unable to make a decision merely because they make an unwise decision

o Any decision or action made on behalf of a person who lacks capacity must be based on their best interests

O  The least intrusive or restrictive action should be pursued wherever possible

## Definition of Lack of Capacity (s.2)

A person lacks capacity in relation to a matter if at the material time he is unable to make a decision for himself in relation to the matter because of an impairment of, or a disturbance in the functioning of, the mind or brain.

A decision as to whether a person lacks capacity has to be decided on the balance of probabilities.

A person is unable to decide for themselves if they are unable (s.3):

O  to understand information relevant to the decision (provided in an accessible manner)

O  to retain that information (even if for only a short period of time)

O  to use or weigh that information as part of the process of making the decision

O  to communicate their decision

## Best Interest

In s.4 this is identified by a number of points. A person making a determination on behalf of a person who lacks capacity must:

O  permit and encourage the person to participate as fully as possible in any decision or act

O  where the decision relates to life saving treatment the decision maker must not be motivated by a desire to bring about their death

O  the decision maker should seek to ascertain:

   -  the persons past and present wishes and feelings
   -  the beliefs and values that would be likely to influence his decision, if he had capacity
   -  any other relevant factor

O    the decision maker should consult:

-    anyone named by the person as someone to be consulted
-    anyone who cares for the person
-    anyone who has been given a Lasting Power of Attorney (LPA) by the person

In doing this, the aim is to identify the person's best interests. Any subsequence decision based on this should be consistent with the spirit of the 2005 Act.

General Authority to Provide Care or Treatment (s.5)

Where a person (D) provides care or treatment for a person (P) then D shall be free from liability (allegations of assault or trespass) if:

O    before engaging in the act (of care or treatment) D takes reasonable steps to establish that P lacks capacity in relation to the particular matter

O    D believes the act is in P's best interests

Then D can engage in the act – termed a "Section 5 act".

Section 6 allows a person caring for someone who lacks capacity to use reasonable restraint where it is necessary to prevent harm to the person who lacks capacity. The restraint must be proportionate and the minimum level must be used.

Lasting Powers of Attorney (LPA) (s.9)

A person (P) can give someone else the authority to make decisions about:

O    P's personal welfare

O    P's property and financial matters

This authority is called a Lasting Power of Attorney.

The LPA is only created if:

O  P is aged 18 or more and has capacity to decide
O  Various conditions have to be met (eg. Form written out, signed, witnessed and lodged with a new office of Public Guardian)

## Court Decisions Making Powers

Civil courts can make declarations for a person who lacks capacity or appoint a person (a deputy) to make decisions on behalf of the person.
It is considered preferable for the court to make a declaration rather than appoint a deputy. (sections 15 to 21)

## Advance Decisions

An individual, while they have capacity, can make a statement stating that they do not wish certain life saving treatments to be given to them if they lose their capacity and that particular situation arises.  If such an advance statement is valid and known by those providing treatment, it must be observed (s.24 to 26). Advance decisions relating to life saving treatment must follow specific guidelines to be valid.

Advance decisions relating to care or treatment that is not essential to save life can be verbal. However the draft code of practice does recommend that advance decisions are written down. If a person makes a verbal advance decision it is best they ensure the key professional knows!

For aspects relating to advance decisions and mental health problems see the section below on the relationship between the Mental Health Act 1983 and the Mental Capacity Act 2005.

## Independent Mental Capacity Advocates

A scheme is established allowing the appointment of Independent Mental Capacity Advocates (IMCA) who will work with individuals who:

O   have no social support network, no family or friends in contact
    with them

O   have to take significant decisions

O   lack capacity

Significant decisions could include serious medical treatment or
moving residence.

Under the Act the Secretary of State for Health is given the duty to
make regulations that will be applied to IMCA services.

The regulations that govern the IMCA service are:

The Mental Capacity Act 2005 (Independent Capacity Advocates)
(General) Regulations 2006 (Ref: 2006 No. 1832).

These regulations are a Statutory Instrument and came into effect on
1st November 2006.  Broadly they regulate the following:

O   How the IMCA will be appointed

O   Role of the IMCA and their ability to challenge decisions

O   Define "serious medical treatment" (from section 36 of the Act)

O   Defines "NHS Body" (from section 37 of the Act)

O   Sets out how the IMCA service will eventually be expanded to
    other groups and situations

O   Costs, training and awareness raising are just some of the other
    issues raised in the regulations

The 2005 Act and the regulations expects IMCA to:

O   support the person who lacks capacity (P) to be as involved as
    fully as possible in decision making

O   gather relevant information

O   identify what P's wishes and feelings would likely be

O   identify alternative courses of action

O    where medical treatment is proposed, obtain a further medical
     opinion if felt necessary

The advocates are to be given the option to challenge any relevant
decisions.

Where an NHS body is going to provide serious medical treatment or
provide accommodation to a person who lacks capacity they must
appoint to the person an IMCA if the person who lacks capacity has
no-one who can speak for them (s.37 and 38).

If a local authority is to provide accommodation for more than 8
weeks or arrange a change in long stay accommodation, then they
must appoint an IMCA if the service user lacks capacity and has no-
one who can speak for them (family or friend) (s.38).

The Regulations are contained in a large document and provide
significant detail.  Interested parties are urged to study them first hand
for further information.

Court of Protection

Although a Court of Protection already exists, the 2005 Act
establishes a new Court of Protection.  It has enhanced powers
including the ability to make directions about the welfare of a person
who lacks capacity.

The Court of Protection has the power to call for reports from NHS
bodies and local authorities.

Public Guardian

This is a new office.  Its role is to:

O    establish and maintain registers of Lasting Powers of Attorney

O    establish a register of orders appointing deputies and supervising
     deputies (appointed by a court)

O    direct Court of Protection Visitors to visit donors or donees of
     LPA's or deputies

o   respond to complaints concerning how an attorney or deputy is exercising their power

The Public Guardian can have access to the health and social care records of an individual, referred to them, who lacks capacity.

The 2005 Act also covers other areas such as research which could involve individuals who lack capacity.

## The Relationship Between the Mental Health Act 1983 and the Mental Capacity Act 2005

It is important to bear in mind that people who are detained under the Mental Health Act 1983 do not necessarily lack capacity when it comes to certain specific decisions. Also most people who lack capacity will never be subject to the provisions of the Mental Health Act 1983.

## Which Act Should Be Used?

o   The Mental Capacity Act 2005 is only relevant to people aged 16 or more who lack capacity to consent at the time a decision needs to be made, or action taken, in connection with the person's care or treatment

o   If the person lacks capacity and treatment is required for a physical health problem the Mental Capacity Act 2005 must be used. The Mental Health Acts of 1983 and 2007 are irrelevant.

o   If treatment is required for a mental disorder and the person still has capacity the Mental Capacity Act 2005 is irrelevant

## Restraint and Detention

The Mental Capacity Act 2005 makes provision for the use of reasonable and proportionate restraint. However this should not be misused and there are situations which would indicate that the Mental Health Act 1983, as amended by the Mental Health Act 2007, should be invoked. Possible situations include:

- It is not possible to provide appropriate care or treatment in a way which does not amount to deprivation of the person's liberty

- The person is resisting treatment and restraint is required regularly or frequently, or for a prolonged period, in order to ensure that they receive treatment.

- There is a risk the person may not receive the treatment and either the person or others might suffer harm as a result.

## People Detained Under the Mental Health Act 1983

When a person is detained under the Mental Health Act 1983 all decisions about the treatment the person receives in respect of their mental health problems are made in line with the existing provisions of the Mental Health Act 1983 as amended by the Mental Health Act 2007.

If a decision needs to be made that is unrelated to treatment for the person's mental health problems (for example the person's physical health, financial or welfare decisions), an assessment must be made of the individuals capacity to make that particular decision at the time it needs to be made. If the person lacked capacity then the provisions of the Mental Capacity Act 2005 apply to that decision or action.

The Mental Capacity Act 2005 makes clear (s.28) that the 2005 Act does not apply to any treatment given to a person under the authority of Part IV of the Mental Health Act 1983 as amended by the Mental Health Act 2007..

## Advanced Decisions

An advance decision to refuse treatment relating to addressing a person's mental health problems is not binding on the health professional when the person has been detained. An advance decision to refuse treatment should be taken into account by the health professionals when deciding whether it is appropriate to provide the treatment for the person's mental health problems, as if it was a contemporaneous refusal of consent by the patient.

The Role of Attorneys or Deputies

Attorneys acting under an LPA or deputies appointed by a court can still make decisions for someone who is detained under the Mental Health Act 1983. However;

o They cannot make decisions about treatment regulated by Part IV of the Mental Health Act 1983.

o Where the service user is subject to guardianship or supervised discharge, the attorney or deputy cannot make decisions that are the responsibility of the guardian or supervisor

A person detained under the Mental Health Act 1983 could create an LPA if they had the capacity to do so.

An attorney or deputy, with the relevant authority, can apply to a Mental Health Review Tribunal to request that the service user is discharged from detention, guardianship or supervised discharge.

**Compulsory Removal of a Person**

Where a person does not have a mental disorder a person can be compulsorily removed from their home under s.47 of the National Assistance Act 1948. Certain conditions have to be met. If a magistrate is satisfied that the conditions do apply to a particular person they can be compulsorily moved into a care home where they have to stay for three months. This requirement can be renewed by the magistrate if necessary.

**Sexual Abuse**

The Sexual Offences Act (SOA) 2003 has updated the laws around sexual offences. Some of the sections of the SOA 2003 amend and re-enact offences that exist already. Other sections introduce new offences aimed at enhancing the protection of the public, whilst some sections introduce offences aimed at protecting vulnerable adults from abuse and exploitation. The SOA 2003 makes most sexual offences gender neutral (they apply to men and women). A few offences are still gender specific.

## Consent

A sexual act between two adults needs to be consensual. The 2003 Act establishes the basis for valid consent.

A person consents if they agree by choice and they have the freedom and capacity to make that choice (s.74).

There are a variety of circumstances that would indicate that if a sexual act occurred it was without consent. These circumstances (at the time of the relevant sexual act) include:

O   there was violence against the victim or the victim was in fear of violence

O   because of communication difficulties the victim could not express consent

O   the victim had been administered, without consent, a substance that results in them being stupefied

[This list is not exhaustive.]

## Rape
*SOA 2003, s.2*

It is an offence for a person (A) to intentionally penetrate with his penis the vagina, anus or mouth of another person (B) without B's consent and A does not reasonably believe that B consents. This is one of the few gender specific offences in the SOA 2003. It applies to men only.

## Assault by penetration
*SOA 2003, s.2*

It is an offence for a person (A) intentionally to penetrate the vagina or anus of another person (B) and B does not consent to the penetration. A does not reasonably believe that B consents. The penetration could involve a finger or object and is for a sexual motive.

## Sexual assault
*SOA 2003, s.3*

It is an offence for a person (A) to intentionally engage in sexual touching of another person (B) without B's consent and A does not reasonably believe that B consents.

## Administering a substance with intent
*SOA 2003, s.61*

It is an offence for a person (A) to intentionally administer a substance, or cause a substance to be taken by another person (B) where A knows that B does not consent to taking the substance and when A intends to stupefy or overpower B for sexual reasons.

## Sex with an adult relative
*SOA 2003 s.64 and s.65*

Together these two sections make it an offence to engage in sexual penetration with someone who is known to be a relative. The list of relatives included has been extended by this Act and includes parents, grandparents, son, daughter, brother, sister, aunt, uncle, niece and nephew. (This list is not comprehensive.)

## Sexual activity in a public lavatory
*SOA 2003, s.71*

It is an offence for a person to engage in sexual activity in a public lavatory.

## Preventing Sexual Abuse and Exploitation of Vulnerable Adults

The following sections of the Sexual Offences Act 2003 are intended to protect adults with a mental disorder from sexual abuse or exploitation.

The definition of mental disorder effectively includes all adults with a mental health problem (this would include a person with dementia) or a learning disability.

## Offences against persons with a mental disorder impeding choice

There are four sections in the SOA 2003 that aim to protect people with a mental health problem or a learning disability who lack the capacity to choose (s.30 to s.33).

A person lacks the capacity to choose if:

O   They are unable to understand the nature of the sexual act or

O   The reasonably foreseeable consequences of the sexual activity

O   Is unable to communicate any choice

O   Or is unable to choose due to any other reason

The range of offences include:

O   Sexual activity (this ranges from sexual touching to penetration) with a person with a mental health problem or a learning disability where the victim lacks the capacity to choose.

O   Causing or inciting a person (A) to engage in sexual activity. This is where A lacks the capacity to choose due to the nature of their mental health problem or learning disability. The sexual activity could be with a third party.

O   Causing a person (A) to watch a sexual act (eg. pornographic film) where A lacks the capacity to choose due to the nature of their mental health problem or learning disability. There is a requirement with this offence that the perpetrator derives sexual gratification from this action.

## Using inducements, threats or deception with an adult with a mental health problem or a learning disability

There are four sections in the SOA 2003 that seek to protect adults who are vulnerable because they have a learning disability or a mental health problem. If an adult with a mental health problem or a learning disability engages in a sexual activity because they were threatened, offered inducements (money, alcohol, drugs etc) or as a result of deception then the perpetrator is committing an offence.

The adult with the mental health problem or learning disability may well be independent and have the capacity to consent to sexual activity. However if the adult with the mental health problem or learning disability agrees to engage in sexual activity due to threats, inducement or deception the person's agreement is seen as not valid – there is no true consent. These offences could be used to protect a service user who is quite independent from being sexually exploited by a neighbour or member of the public.

The range of offences (s.34 to s.37) includes

O   Using inducement, threat or deception to engage in sexual activity with a person with a mental health problem or a learning disability

O   Using inducement, threat or deception to cause a person with a mental health problem or a learning disability to engage in sexual activity (with a third party).

O   Using inducement, threat or deception to cause a person with a mental health problem or a learning disability to watch a sexual act (such as watch a pornographic film) so that the perpetrator gets sexual gratification.

### Protecting service users with a mental health problem or a learning disability from sexual exploitation by staff

The Sexual Offences Act 2003 uses the term care worker. This is defined so broadly that it includes all staff who work with service users who have a mental health problem or a learning disability. Hence the term care worker includes consultants, G.P.'s, nurses (community or hospital based), social workers, residential staff, day service staff, community care workers and all support staff who work in services.

The service user may well have the capacity to agree to engage in sexual activity. However, if the sexual activity is with a member of staff any agreement by the service user is seen as invalid. There is no real consent. There is an assumption that the member of staff has abused their position of trust.

The offences under the SOA 2003 (s.38 to s.41) include:

o   Sexual activity between a member of staff and a service user with a mental health problem or a learning disability. The sexual activity can be anything from sexual touching to penetration.

o   A staff member causing or inciting a service user with a mental health problem or a learning disability to engage in sexual activity with a third party. This is intended to stop a staff member exploiting his or her position of trust as a 'pimp' or equivalent.

o   A staff member causing a service user with a mental health problem or a learning disability to watch a sexual act, such that the staff member obtains sexual gratification.

This last section is not intended to prevent legitimate sex education. In providing sex education as part of an approved care plan a staff member or professional should not derive sexual gratification.

All the offences relating to protecting people with a learning disability or a mental health problem are gender neutral. They apply equally to men and women.

### Protecting Vulnerable Adults from Harassment and Physical Abuse

All adults have the right to be free from the fear of violence. Therefore vulnerable adults can look to receiving the same protection in law as anyone else can claim in respect of physical violence.

There is evidence that some people with learning disabilities and some people with mental health problems have been subjected to street abuse, harassment and intimidation, both in the street and when they are at home. Staff should support vulnerable adults make complaints to the police, possibly through initial contact with Community Support Officers. Community Support Officer's role is to enhance community safety although they have fewer powers than the police.

Consideration should be given to whether Anti-Social behaviour Orders (ASBO's) could protect the vulnerable adult, as well as considering other criminal or civil law options.

**Any individual who ill treats a mentally disordered person who is in their custody or care (whether by virtue of any legal or moral obligation or otherwise)**
*Mental Health Act 1983 s.127 (2)*

This could be used to protect any person with mental health problems or who has a learning disability. Ill treatment includes abuse where no injury is involved. It could include verbal harassment.

## Domestic Violence

The Government has highlighted the importance of responding assertively to domestic violence and expects all agencies to co-ordinate their response. Readers are advised to see a copy of the policy document "Domestic Violence: Break The Chain. Multi-Agency Guidance for Addressing Domestic Violence" (Home Office 2000).

There are a number of Acts that are relevant when considering how to respond to domestic violence or abuse.

## Family Law Act 1996

Part IV of this Act relates to protecting a person from domestic abuse. This Part of the Act has been strengthened by sections inserted by the Domestic Violence, Crime and Victims Act 2004.
The civil court actions that a person can take to protect themselves consists of applying for

- a non-molestation order. A court can require a person who has been 'associated' with the victim to stop engaging in violent, threatening or pestering behaviour. A person who breaches a non-molestation order commits an offence, and so could be arrested by the police and face a prison sentence, if convicted.

- occupation order. A person who has been 'associated' with an individual, such that they shared a common home either as a married couple or cohabiting partners, can apply for a occupation order in respect of the shared home. The court can make an occupation order if certain conditions are satisfied; these include that the applicant is likely to suffer harm due to the behaviour of their partner (or ex-partner) if the order is not made. Powers of arrest can also be attached to the order.

Occupation orders are inclusive and apply to married couples and co-habitating couples (whether heterosexual couples or same sex couples).

**Protection from Harassment Act 1997**

A person who is subjected to harassment or intimidatory pestering can seek protection through both the criminal and civil courts.

**Housing Act 1996**

This Act imposes on local authorities a duty to house people who are unintentionally homeless and in priority need. The duty to house people who are unintentionally homeless has been strengthened by the Homelessness Act 2002. The original 1996 Act applied a duty to house people for a period of two years. After that housing authorities were able (but not obliged) to continue to secure accommodation. The Homelessness Act 2002 removes this time limit. The duty to secure accommodation is discharged when the circumstances that led to being accepted as homeless are addressed.

Section 177 of the 1996 Act is also amended. This particular section relates to people claiming to be homeless who are at risk of violence. The 2002 Act established that it is not reasonable for a person to continue to occupy accommodation if it is probable that this will lead to violence or threats of violence against them or someone with whom they usually reside.

**Forced Marriage (Civil Protection) Act 2007**
Territorial Extent: England, Wales (Northern Ireland in part)

This Act received Royal Assent on 26th July 2007. It amends the Family Law Act 1996, the Supreme Court Act 1981, the Courts and Legal Services Act 1990, the Family Homes and Domestic Violence Order (N.I.) 1998 and the Access to Justice (N.I.) Order 2003.

The Act provides civil remedies for those facing forced marriage and victims of forced marriage.

A court may make a Forced Marriage Protection order which offers three-way protection:

o   To protect a person from being forced into marriage

o   Prevent any attempt to force a person into marriage

o   Protect a person who has been forced into marriage

The Act places the well-being, wishes and feelings of the subject/ victim at the centre of the proceedings and also defines the meaning of forced marriage. The Act also sets out the scope of what constitutes coercion into marriage including, interestingly, a threat of suicide by the perpetrator. Clearly the Act has responded to consultation and taken account of cultural factors.

As an alternative to an order, the court may accept an "undertaking", or promise, from the respondent (alleged perpetrator). However, the court has the same powers of response to the breach of an undertaking as with breach of an order. This seems a fair way to apply the "no order" principle. The Act also contains supporting legislation relating to varying orders, powers of arrest etc and further study of the Act and its guidance is recommended, if this is applicable to your working practice.

**Criminal Law**

Anyone who is subjected to domestic violence has the same rights to seek protection from the police and the criminal justice system as anyone else who is subjected to similar violence committed against them by a complete stranger.

 **In Summary**

The Government has made clear that it wants to promote the personal security of all people. Policy initiatives to protect vulnerable adults are aimed at encouraging co-ordinated multi-agency responses.

# 10 THE PROVISION OF COMMUNITY CARE SERVICES

So far we have looked at legislation in terms of areas of practice. There are however, a number of specific pieces of legislation which you need to know about. Some of these we have already covered in parts of previous sections. In this chapter we give more information on the following specific legislation:-

O   National Assistance Act 1948
O   Chronically Sick and Disabled Persons Act 1970
O   Local Authority Social Services Act 1970
O   National Health Service Act 1977
O   The Health and Social Services and Social Security Adjudication Act 1983
O   Mental Health Act 1983
O   Disabled Persons (Services, Consultation and Representation) Act 1986
O   Health and Medicines Act 1988
O   NHS and Community Care Act 1990
O   Carers (Recognition and Services) Act 1995
O   Mental Health (Patients in the Community) Act 1995
O   Community Care (Direct Payments) Act 1996
O   Health Act 1999
O   Health and Social Care Act 2001
O   Community Care (Delayed Discharges etc) Act 2003
O   Domestic, Violence, Crime and Victims Act 2004
O   Mental Capacity Act 2005
O   National Health Service Act 2006
O   National Health Service (Consequential Provisions) Act 2006
O   National Health Service (Redress) Act 2006
O   National Health Service (Wales) Act 2006
O   Mental Health Act 2007

We have covered these pieces of legislation in chronological order, they are not arranged in order of importance or relevance to practice etc.

## National Assistance Act 1948

Whilst this is an old Act, various aspects of community care services are still defined by this Act.

Section 21 makes it a duty of the local authority to provide (or arrange) residential care for anyone aged 18 or over who by reason of age, illness, disability or other circumstances are in need of such care and this care is not otherwise available.

The use of the term 'other circumstances' has been used to formally include individuals with alcohol or drug related dependency and expectant or nursing mothers.

Where a person enters residential care s.22 imposes a duty on the local authority to conduct a financial assessment of the service-users ability to pay for that service. Where the resident is able too they must pay the full cost of the care.

Section 29 gives local authorities the power to provide services to people aged 18 or over who have care needs as a result of a mental health problem, a physical or learning disability or who are blind or deaf.

## Chronically Sick and Disabled Persons Act 1970

Section 1 of this Act places a duty on local authorities to ascertain the number of chronically sick and disabled persons in its area and to publicise the services provided for them.

The Act imposes a duty on social services to provide the following services for people ordinarily resident in their area where it is necessary to meet their needs:-

O  provide for practical assistance in the home

O  provide recreational and educational facilities outside the home

O  provide facilities or assistance in travelling to/from home to participant in any provided services

O  provide adaptations to the home

o   provide additional facilities in the home designed to secure greater safety, comfort or convenience

o   facilitate the taking of holidays

o   facilitate meals in the home or elsewhere

o   provide a telephone and any special equipment necessary to enable the person to use a telephone.

This Act applies to people of all ages although in practice it is often difficult for people over the age of 60 to achieve registration under the Act.

The Act is generous in provision.  However in practice you may find that many such services are not provided under the current financial climate.

**Local Authority Social Services Act 1970**

This Act established local authority social services departments.  As a result of amendments the local authority is required to establish a director adult social care services and a director of childrens social care services (effectively creating two social services departments, one for adults, one for children).  Significant sections of this Act relate to establishing the local authority social services committee.

Section 7 makes clear that local authorities, in exercising their social services functions shall act under the general guidance of the Secretary of State [hence Department of Health guidance is issued under s.7 of this Act].

**National Health Service Act 1977**

This Act places a duty of co-operation between local health authorities and social services departments.  The 1977 Act has been further strengthened by the Health Act 1999.  The Health Act amended parts of the 1977 Act relating to co-operation between NHS bodies and local authorities.

In Schedule 8 of this Act the local authority is given the power to provide services to adults for the purpose of preventing illness or to prevent the break-up of families.

## Mental Health Act 1983

This Act has been significantly amended by the Mental Health Act 2007 – see pages 93-95. This is a very wide ranging and complex piece of legislation. We give here only a <u>very</u> brief outline. If you need more information it is important that you refer to the Act as there are a number of complexities within the legislation.

The Act is supplemented by an associated Code of Practice, which is periodically updated.

The definitions of mental disorder which are contained in Section 1 of the Act are of central importance as this Act only applies to people who are believed to be "mentally disordered."

A broad definition of mental disorder is given as:

*"mental illness, arrested or incomplete development of mind, psychopathic disorder and any other disorder or disability of mind"*

The Act refers to Approved Social Workers (ASW's) - it states that a local authority must appoint a sufficient number of ASW's and refers to the process of Approving Social Workers under the Act.

The main sections of the Act refer to admissions to hospital. Compulsory admissions can be made to hospital following an application by an Approved Social Worker or the person's *nearest relative*. The nearest relative is not necessarily the person's next of kin and specific details are given in the Act. In practice the majority of applications are made by ASW's.

In brief a person can be compulsorily admitted to hospital for:-

O  Assessment - Section 2 (maximum of 28 days)

O  Treatment - Section 3 (maximum six months, renewable for six months and thereafter for one year periods)

| Section Number | Purpose | Duration |
|---|---|---|
| 2 | Admission for assessment | 28 days. Not renewable |
| 3 | Admission for treatment | 6 months. May be renewed for six months, then yearly |
| 4 | Admission for assessment in an emergency | 72 hours. Not renewable - but can be changed to Section 2 |
| 5 (2) | Doctors holding power | 72 hours. Not renewable |
| 5 (4) | Nurses holding power | 6 hours. Not renewable but a doctor can change to section 5(2) |
| 7 | Reception into guardianship | 6 months. May be renewed for 6 months, then yearly |
| 35 | Remand to hospital for psychiatric report | 28 days, court may renew 28 days at a time up to a maximum of 12 weeks |
| 36 | Remand to hospital for psychiatric treatment | As above. |
| 37 | Hospital Order (Court) | 6 months. May be renewed for 6 months then yearly |
| 135 | Warrant to search for and remove a patient | 72 hours - not renewable |
| 136 | Police power to move a person to a place of safety from a public place | 72 hours - not renewable |

The Act also outlines Guardianship orders. These are of six months duration, they can be renewed for six months and thereafter for one year periods. If the application for guardianship is accepted then a named person or a social services department is named as the person's "guardian". The named guardian has the following powers:-

O    to require the person to reside at a specified place

O    to require the person to attend medical treatment, occupation, education or training as specified

O    to require access to the person by an ASW, medical practitioner or other specified person

These are the main sections of the Act which make reference to admissions.

However, as stated, there are a number of complex areas covered within the Act. The table on page 85 outlines the main sections of the Act, their purpose and duration.

The Mental Health Act also covers Mental Health Review Tribunals. There is a Tribunal for each Regional Health Authority and each consists of legal members, medical members and lay members. Sections 66-78 of the Act refer to tribunals. Basically, however, patients are able to appeal to tribunals at various points during compulsory hospital stays.

The final major area covered by the Act is covered in s.117. This states that the local health authority and social services have a duty to provide after care services for people for whom the section is relevant. For this reason you may hear people referred to as "Section 117 eligible."

The Mental Health (Patients in the Community) Act 1995 inserted additional sections into the 1983 Act. Several of these new sections relate to After-Care under supervision.

A patient can be placed on supervised aftercare if certain conditions are met these include:-

o   the person has a specified mental disorder

o   there is a substantial risk of serious harm to the patient or someone else if the after care was not supervised

o   receiving supervised aftercare is likely to ensure the patient receives the necessary services

A patient on supervised aftercare can have certain conditions placed on them which they are required to observe e.g. live at a specified place, attend specified places for treatment, occupation etc.

## Health and Social Services and Social Security Adjudication Act 1983

This Act states that if a person who is in receipt of services transfers their capital to another person (eg: relative) then any beneficiary is liable to repay the funds in order that charges can be met.
The power to charge for community care services (i.e. all except residential care) is derived from s.17 of this Act.

## Disabled Persons (Services, Consultation and Representation) Act 1986

This Act began as a private members bill, and much of it has never been implemented. Some of the sections that were implemented in 1987 include:-

Section 4 requires the local authority to consider the needs of a disabled person in an assessment, whilst section 8 states that the local authority has a duty to take account of a carer's ability to continue to provide support to the person at the point of assessment.

Section 9 states that the local authority must inform disabled people about all services which may be available to them - not just those provided by the local authority.

Section 10 states that organisations of disabled people must be consulted before the appointment of any person to a council, committee or body on which members with special knowledge of disabled people are statutorily required.

## Health and Medicines Act 1988

This gives health authorities and NHS Trusts the power to charge for supplies. For example, if any NHS Trust provides routine incontinence aids to a nursing home the Trust can charge the home for these supplies.

## National Health Service and Community Care Act 1990

The philosophy underlying the Act is that of a user orientated service offering flexible and efficient matching of services to service user

---

needs. The concept of partnership between social services departments, the NHS, voluntary organisations concerned with health and welfare and private organisations is one of the keys to success of the legislation. The primary focus of the Act is the reform of the organisation and funding of social care.

The White Paper, Caring for People outlined six objectives for social services departments.

1. To promote the development of domiciliary, day and respite services, to enable people to live in their own homes wherever feasible and sensible.

2. To ensure that service purchasers make practical support for carers a high priority.

3. To make proper assessment of need and good care management the cornerstone of high quality care.

4. To promote the development of a flourishing independent sector alongside good quality public services

5. To clarify the responsibilities of agencies and so make it easier to hold them to account for their performance.

6. To secure better value for taxpayers' money by introducing a new funding system for social care.

*Duty to Assess*

The NHS and Community Care Act specifies the duty of the local authority to carry out assessment of an individual's care needs. As a result of this assessment the local authority will decide whether the person's needs are such that they require a service.

To conduct these assessments of need the new role of care manager was created. Following the assessment of an individual's needs, care management tasks include planning and arranging for the provision of packages of care; monitoring the quality of services provided and reviewing the service-user's needs.

Care packages should foster the independence of the individual and should be constructed with the active involvement of service-users, their carers, and, where appropriate, an advocate.

## Intentions of the Act

The Act sought to ensure that services develop flexibly to meet individual's needs and change to meet the broader social care needs of the community.

For people who do require services it was intended that they should be able to have a choice about the service/s they will eventually receive.

Additionally, all service-users and carers have, in effect, been given the right to comment about the services provided. Each local authority has established comments and complaints procedure. This has to be widely publicised by each local authority.

Any one individual may receive services from several organisations. These should be delivered in a co-ordinated way - with the hope that they would be, in effect, a seamless service.

All services should be of a high quality. Inspection services were reformed. Since then regulation and inspection has gone through far more significant changes.

The Act was largely concerned with establishing a system that used public resources efficiently. As part of this it established the purchaser/provider split. Within adult services care managers/social worker represent the purchasers who can buy services from any provider (residential services/day services/home care).

## Mental Health (Patients in the Community) Act 1995

The principle sections of this Act that relate to England and Wales are inserted into the Mental Health Act 1983. The Mental Health (Patients in the Community) Act introduced aftercare under supervision.

## Carers (Recognition and Services) Act 1995

This Act places a duty on social services departments to carry out an assessment of carer's needs.

Where an assessment is being carried out under the NHS and Community Care Act 1990 a carer may request that, before making a decision, an assessment of their needs and ability to continue to provide care is carried out.

## Community Care (Direct Payments) Act 1996

This Act originally introduced direct payments as an option for social services. The sections of this Act that relate to England have all been repealed. The legislative basis of direct payments is now the Health and Social Care Act 2001.

## Health Act 1999

This Act reinforced the importance of NHS bodies and local authorities co-operating in the delivery of services that could result in enhancing the health of people they are responsible for. As an expression of this the Act allows for joint funding of services.

## Health and Social Care Act 2001

This Act introduced the possibility of NHS organisations (a Primary Care Trust or a NHS Trust) entering into a partnership with a local authority to form a Care Trust so that the health and social care needs of the local population would be met by the one Care Trust (s.45). This Act also gives the Secretary of State the power to direct that a Care Trust is established if a local NHS organisation or a local authority are failing to perform their services adequately (s.46).

Through s.57 of this Act the Secretary of State is given the power to make regulations requiring local authorities to offer direct payments to all adults who satisfy certain conditions and whose social care needs meet the eligibility criteria.

Direct payments involves the social services department giving the service user money, instead of arranging services. With this money the service user can employ staff so that their care needs can be met or can purchase support time with a care provider of their choice.

Direct payments cannot be made to:-

O   some people with mental health problems (eg. on supervised discharge)

O   some people who are dependent on alcohol/drugs

The Government is very keen for direct payments to be widely taken up.  They want more service users (across the board) to have direct payments.

**Community Care (Delayed Discharges, etc) Act 2003**

This Act gives health organisations the power to charge local authorities when an NHS patient's discharge from hospital is delayed because social services have not completed an assessment and/or arranged any services that are required to facilitate discharge. The charge can only be levied when the social services department is responsible for any delay.

The NHS organisation, usually an NHS Trust will need to give the social services department notice that a patient is likely to need care services on discharge. This known as a 'section 2 notice' – since it is section 2 of the Act.

The length of time that social services will have to assess the patient and arrange services will depend on how early the section 2 notice is given. The minimum notice that will be allowable is stated in regulations. However, the Act does indicate a minimum level that any regulations could go to. This is three days (with the day the section 2 notice is given counting as the first day).

**National Health Service Act 2006**
Territorial Extent: England

This is very much an administrative Act, which addresses the role of various authorities including the Secretary of State, Strategic Health Authorities, Primary Care Trusts, NHS Trusts and other Health Authorities.  Finance and charging are also discussed.  Sections 4 to 7 detail various duties to provide medical and dental, ophthalmic and pharmaceutical services, while part 8 discusses the family Services Appeal Authority.

The Act may be of use to advocates, but otherwise it appears to offer little information of use to staff in a direct care role.

### National Health Service (Consequential Provisions) Act 2006
Territorial Extent: England and Wales

This is an Act very much concerned with tidying previous legislation and consolidating the NHS Act 2006 and the NHS Act (Wales) 2006. It contains little that is of relevance to direct care staff.

### National Health Service (Redress) Act 2006
Territorial Extent: England and Wales

This Act allows for the provision of a redress scheme to, essentially, compensate people who suffer harm as a result of services provided by the NHS in England or Wales. This is intended to avoid the need for civil legal proceedings. The proposed scheme is concerned with giving compensation but also giving explanations, apologies and providing report information to ensure the same mistake is not repeated.

The Act also makes provision for free legal advice for claimants and its general thrust is to work towards resolution, rather than in a purely adversarial way.

This Act is not a scheme or set of rights in itself, rather it enables the Secretary of State to set up a scheme.

### National Health Service (Wales) Act 2006
Territorial Extent: Wales

This Act consolidates certain enactments relating to the Health Services in Wales and its inter-relation with England. There is little to inform direct care staff, but it defines Welsh Ministers' authority in the running of healthcare provision at many levels and for a range of services.

## Mental Health Act 2007

This Act received Royal Assent on 19th July 2007. It amends the Mental Health Act 1983 the Mental Capacity Act 2005 and the Domestic Violence, Crime and Victims Act 2004

This Act amends the legislation governing the compulsory treatment of people with a mental disorder which is laid out in the Mental Health Act 1983. The 2007 Act also introduces "deprivation of liberty safeguards" by amending the Mental Capacity Act 2005 in response to the "Bournewood Judgement". It also amends the Domestic Violence Crime and Victims Act 2004 by extending the rights of victims.

The Act covers the covers the territorial areas of the Acts it amends – mainly England and Wales, although it also updates legislation for the transfer of patients between all UK areas.

<u>1983 Mental Health Act – Main Changes</u>

o *Definition of Mental Disorder:* applies a new, single definition. The new, simpler definition for the purpose of legislation is "any disorder or disability of the mind". Previous definitions are removed from the 1983 Act. The redundant definitions, now omitted from the 1983 Act are "mental illness, arrested or incomplete development of mind, psychopathic disorder or any other disorder or disability of mind".

o *Young People and Age Appropriate Treatment:* Patients under 18 must be provided with accommodation that is suitable to their age. Duty rests with hospital managers. Also young people aged 16 to 17 who either consent or refuse treatment cannot have their decision overruled by an adult who has parental responsibility for them.

o *Criteria for Detention:* New "Appropriate Medical Treatment" test introduced, meaning that the patient cannot be detained unless appropriate medical treatment is available for them. The old "treatability test" is abolished.

o *Professional Roles:* broadens the range of professionals who can take on the roles previously only carried out by Approved Social

Workers (ASW) and the Responsible Medical Officer (RMO). The ASW role is now reclassified as the Approved Mental Health Professional (AMHP) and for this role social workers, nursing staff, occupational therapists or psychologists may be eligible for Approved status. The AMHP assumes the role of initially applying for admission and detention of patients under Part 2 of the 1983 Act. The RMO role is replaced by the Responsible Clinician (RC) also referred to as an "approved clinician" in the 2007 Act. The same group of professionals listed above, in addition to registered medical practitioners, can be approved for this role.

O *Nearest Relative:* new right for patients and county courts to apply to displace the nominated nearest relative. Also, Civil Partners added to the list of relatives.

O *Supervised Community Treatment (SCT):* New for patients following a period of hospital detention. Aimed at tackling the "revolving door" of readmission following treatment failure in the community.

O *Mental Health Review Tribunal:* New power to reduce the time before hospital managers must refer the case to a tribunal. New single tribunal for England.

O *Advocacy:* Independent Mental Health Advocates must be available.

O *Electro Convulsive Therapy:* New patient safeguards are introduced which relate to the patient's ability to consent and to understand the nature and effects of treatment. A patient cannot be given ECT unless they have consented and an approved clinician (or registered medical practitioner if under 18) has certified that they are capable of understanding and giving consent. Where a patient does not have the understanding to give informed consent a registered medical practitioner must certify that the patient is not capable of understanding the nature of the treatment, and that it is appropriate treatment in the circumstances. This must not conflict with any valid "advance decision" or a decision by the Court of Protection.

## Domestic, Violence, Crime and Victims Act 2004 – Main changes

New rights for victims of offenders who are mentally disordered but not subject to any restrictions. Victims can make representations to receive information about discharge dates, treatment and conditions. There is also a framework for them to have input into the decision making process when deciding conditions.

Mental Health rights is a large area of some peoples work and we would advise reviewing the text and guidance of this Act directly if you require further information.

## Mental Capacity Act 2005 - Main changes

Procedures are introduced to detain someone who is already in a hospital/care home but who does not have the capacity to give consent. This is important because a person cannot be given compulsory treatment if they agree to receive treatment anyway. What do you do when a person can neither consent or decline? These new procedures carry over the values of the Mental Capacity Act 2005 – to act in the persons best interests, in the least restrictive manner.

 **In Summary**

Many people have criticised the NHS and Community Care Act 1990, since it did not replace much of the previous legislation in this area. This means that the NHS and Community Care Act must be viewed in conjunction with a variety of other legislation.

**STANDARDS IN SOCIAL CARE**

The Care Standards Act 2000 introduced significant changes and new institutions. The scope of its reforms required implementation to be staggered over two to three years.

One of the new institutions established was the National Care Standards Commission (NCSC). This was the new inspection body for all care homes and domiciliary care agencies in England. The NCSC became operational in April 2002. In mid April 2002 the Secretary of State for Health announced that the NCSC would be abolished and replaced with a new organisation called the Commission for Social Care Inspection (CSCI). To establish this new Commission (the CSCI) further legislation would be required. The Health and Social Care (Community Health and Standards) Act 2003 was the legislative vehicle by which the CSCI was established.

Most of the Care Standards Act 2000 is still valid. All of the duties of the (now disbanded) NCSC in respect of inspecting organisations providing social care have been transferred to the CSCI.

The CSCI is due to be broken up and disbanded in 2008! The responsibility for inspecting social care services for adults will be transferred to the Healthcare Commission.

In this chapter the Care Standards Act 2000 will still be discussed but where it has been amended by more recent legislation this will also be included in the text.

## Care Services

The Care Standards Act 2000 defines a whole range of care services. A care home is defined as any home which provides accommodation together with personal care or nursing care for any person who is ill, or has a disability or is infirm, or has a mental health problem or has an alcohol or drug related dependency (s.3).

A domiciliary care agency is an agency that supplies staff who provide personal care for people in their own homes. (Children's homes and adoption and fostering agencies are also defined.)

## Inspection of Services

All care services as defined by the Care Standards Act must register with the Commission for Social Care Inspection (CSCI).

The Department of Health is given the responsibility of writing regulations (Statutory Instruments) and National Minimum Standards (NMS). The NMS are the 'measure' that the CSCI actively use when they inspect care providers. National Minimum Standards have been written such that they apply to specific service sectors. Therefore there are:

NMS – Older Peoples Residential Care
NMS – Residential Care for Adults aged 18-65
NMS – Domiciliary Care Agencies

The staff of the CSCI who are appointed as inspectors have powers to inspect care establishments and agencies. As part of the inspection process the inspectors can look at all relevant documents and records, interview staff in private and meet with service-users in private (if the service-user agrees to this) (s.31).

This Act makes provision for the future registration and regulation of other care services, notably day centres and day services (s.42).

## General Social Care Council

The Care Standards Act 2000 also establishes an agency titled the General Social Care Council. It is the responsibility of this Council to compile registers of social care workers. Due to the high number of workers in this field it will gradually build up its registers. Priorities in its first few years will be

O   register qualified social workers

O   register staff in children's services

O   register managers of all care homes

To protect the title "social worker" it will become an offence for a person to use this title if they are not registered (s.61).

It is a duty of the Council to produce codes of practice for all social care workers and employers of such staff (s.62). This code of practice has been written and is widely available.

The General Social Care Council will also have the responsibility of supporting the development and regulation of training for all staff in social care in collaboration with Skills for Care.

### Protection of Children and Vulnerable Adults

Part VII of the Care Standards Act 2000 gives the Secretary of State the duty and powers to establish and operate a register of persons considered unsuitable to work with vulnerable adults.

Providers of direct care services to vulnerable adults have a duty to refer social care workers to the Secretary of State for inclusion on this list if the worker, acted in a manner that would constitute "misconduct which harmed or risked harm to a vulnerable adult" (HMSO 2000) (s.82).

Employment agencies also have a duty to refer social care staff they employ to the register on the same grounds of misconduct.

An individual could be referred to the register by other routes e.g. as a result of an inspection by the Commission for Social Care Inspection.

Employers have a duty to check to see if any prospective new employee is on this register.

Any person listed on the protection of vulnerable adults list is automatically included on the Protection of Children Act (1999) list

Individuals referred for inclusion on the protection of vulnerable adults list have a right of appeal against the decision by the Secretary of State to include them on the list. The Secretary of State can remove the names of individuals from the list if the appeal is successful.

Various sections of Part VII of the Care Standards Act amend the Protection of Children Act, so that the operating systems for the protection of vulnerable adults list and the Protection of Children Act list are very similar.

## Health and Social Care (Community Health and Standards) Act 2003

This Act establishes various new public bodies. One of these is the Commission for Social Care Inspection (CSCI). This Commission has merged the Social Services Inspectorate (which used to be based in the Department of Health) with the social care functions of the National Care Standards Commission.

This will mean there is one organisation that inspects social services and social care providers of services.

Under its responsibilities to inspect local authority social services the CSCI has to encourage improvement and to assess performance in relation to a number of measures. These include:

O   Availability and access to services

O   Quality and effectiveness of services

O   The management of services

**O**   The economy and efficiency of their provision and their value for money

Each year the CSCI must award a performance rating to each social services department. The criteria they will use will be devised by the Secretary of State.

The CSCI has also taken over the functions of the National Care Standards Commission relating to inspecting registered social care services (e.g. care homes and domiciliary care agencies). The NCSC has been disbanded – most staff moved to the CSCI.

The functions of the National Care Standards Commission relating to inspecting independent hospitals and independent clinics has been transferred to a new agency, the Commission for Healthcare Audit and Inspection (CHAI) which this (2003) Act established.

### In Summary

The Care Standards Act 2000 introduced initiatives which, have had a significant impact on nearly all care services.

Arguably the most notable aspects are the National Minimum Standards that each care service must achieve and the inspection process.

# 12  SPECIFIC MISCELLANEOUS LEGISLATION

This section discusses legislation that is not specifically focused on social care but in its application it does have implications that are relevant to health and social care.

The Acts covered in this chapter are:

O   Misuse of Drugs Act 1971
O   Police and Criminal Evidence Act 1984
O   Public Interest Disclosure Act 1998
O   Racial and Religious Hatred Act 2006
O   Immigration, Asylum and Nationality Act 2006
O   Health Act 2006
O   Local Government and Public Involvement Act 2007
O   Work and Families Act 2006
O   Sustainable Communities Act 2007
O   Welfare Reform Act 2007
O   Criminal Justice and Immigration Bill 2007/2008

## Misuse of Drugs Act 1971

This Act is the major piece of legislation in Britain relating to the use/misuse of drugs.

A variety of drugs are listed and categorised into Class A, B or C depending on how harmful the drug is.  Any drug which is prepared to be injected is automatically put into Class A.  People who possess or supply Class A drugs risk the most severe penalties for drug misuse - ranging from a fine to life imprisonment.

It is important for staff to be aware of this Act because it is an offence under the Act to knowingly tolerate the use of drugs on premises over which you have control.  This may therefore be relevant to staff working in any social care establishment.

## Police and Criminal Evidence Act 1984

This Act outlines the duties and powers of the police.  It is particularly relevant in terms of social care work with adults to be aware of what is said about vulnerable people.

*The Appropriate Adult*

The code of practice which accompanies the Act recognises two groups as being vulnerable:-

O    juveniles (under 17)

O    people with learning disabilities or mental health problems

The police are expected to treat a person as being vulnerable if there is any doubt.  Where a person falls into a vulnerable category they should be supported by an appropriate adult during police interviews.  In the case of a vulnerable adult an appropriate adult means:-

a)    a relative, guardian or other person responsible for the individual's care or custody.

b)    a person who has experience in work with people with a learning disability or mental health problem, but not someone who is employed by the police. Often this will be a social worker.

c)  failing the above another responsible adult who is not employed by the police.

When a vulnerable person is detained the police should inform the appropriate adult as soon as practicable of the reason for the detention, where the person is being detained and to request that they come to the police station. The person should not then be interviewed in the absence of the appropriate adult.

## Powers of Detention

The Police and Criminal Evidence Act gives police the power to hold an arrested suspect for up to 24 hours from the time of arrival at the police station for the purpose of obtaining evidence. This period can be extended up to a maximum of 36 hours on the authority of a high ranking officer (at least a superintendent).

## Public Interest Disclosure Act 1998

This is often referred to as the "whistle-blowers" legislation. It was implemented in July 1999. This Act gives significant statutory protection to employees who disclose malpractice reasonably and responsibly in the public interest and are victimised as a result. If an employee is victimised or dismissed for this disclosure they can make a claim for compensation to an industrial tribunal. There is no cap to the amount that can be awarded.

Whilst it is not a statutory requirement there is an expectation that organisations will establish their own whistle blowing policy and guidelines. These guidelines should:

O   clearly indicate how staff can raise concerns about malpractice

O   make a clear organisational commitment to take concerns seriously and to protect people from victimisation

O   designate a senior manager with specific responsibility for addressing concerns in confidence which need to be handled outside the usual management-chain

Staff receive the full protection of the Act if they seek to disclose malpractice responsibly e.g. by following the organisations whistle-blowing policy/guidelines.

If a member of staff goes to the media or police first they only receive the statutory protection if certain conditions are met.

### Racial and Religious Hatred Act 2006
Territorial extent: England and Wales

This Act received Royal Assent on 16th February 2006. It amends the Public Order Act 1986 and the Police and Criminal Evidence Act 1984.

This Act creates a new offence of "stirring up hatred against persons on religious grounds", amending the Public Order Act 1986. This offence can be committed through spoken and written words or broadcasting video or audio recording. The intent must be to stir up religious hatred against a group of people on grounds of religious belief or lack of it. Clearly the legislation is not just aimed at the traditional sources of religious hatred – nationalist groups – but also at the activities of radical religious groups themselves.

The Police and Criminal Evidence Act (PACE) 1984 is amended so that there is no power of citizens arrest for this offence. Only a constable has the power to arrest a suspect for this offence. This would appear to be a measure to curb the activities of would be vigilantes.

The Act is not intended to curb free speech and makes provision for making this clear. Neither is promoting a religion or seeking to covert others illegal. Fair and accurate reports of activities are also not seen as an offence. Therefore, for example, reporting on a religiously motivated terrorist attack, which would anger the public, is not "stirring up racial hatred" within the meaning of the Act.

## Immigration, Asylum and Nationality Act 2006

This Act received Royal Assent on 30th March 2006. It amends the Immigration, Asylum and Nationality Act 2002.

This Act is, in some ways, outside the remit of this book. However, as the needs of migrant workers form an increasing part of the social care task load, awareness of this legislation becomes ever more appropriate.

The Act forms part of the Government's five year strategy for asylum and immigration and is divided into four main areas:

O Appeals

O Employment

O Information

O Claimants and Applicants

We advise you to study this Act, or perhaps more usefully, the explanatory notes that go with it, if immigration or asylum issues affect your work. The Act and its guidance can be found via www.opsi.gov.uk.

## Health Act 2006

This Act bundles together several topics within the scope of public health which has aroused public concern. Broadly, the Act aims to protect public health and improve the running of the NHS.

This is the Act that made England and Wales "smoke free" by banning smoking in enclosed and "substantially enclosed" spaces (as the Act puts it). There are even provisions to amend the Merchant Shipping Act to create smoke free ships (great for the nerves in a force 10 gale).

Part 2 of the Act is concerned with the prevention and control of what are called "health associated infections" – hospital bugs to the rest of us. The Act gives the Secretary of State powers to issue a code of practice to combat these. This was fully revised in January 2008 as

Code of Practice for the prevention and control of healthcare associated infections. This code of practice forms part of an NHS body's duty of care under the Health and Social Care (Community Health and Standards) Act 2003.

Other areas covered by the Act are:

O  Management of controlled drugs, in response to the Shipman Enquiry

O  Provision of Pharmacy and ophthalmic services

O  Combating NHS fraud

**Local Government and Public Involvement Act 2007**
Territorial Extent: England and Wales

This Act received Royal Assent on 30th October 2007. It amends the National Health Service Act 2006.

The present Government is committed to local government reform, particularly concerning public involvement in health and social care services. Such white papers as "Strong and Prosperous Communities", "Our Health, Our Care, Our Say" and "A Stronger Local Voice" have contributed to the content of this Act.

Whilst it is not strictly concerned with the details of direct care, Part 14 is entitled "Patient and public involvement in health and social care".

Part 14 abolishes the Patients' forums promoted by the National Health Service Act 2006. Instead it places a duty on both local authorities and Strategic Health Authorities to commission formal arrangements to involve the public and therefore service users, in consultation and planning of health and social services. The Act informally calls these "local involvement networks".

There will be some sort of duty, to be regulated by the Secretary of State, for authorities to respond to requests, reports and recommendations made by local involvement networks and to allow them access to information.

The Commission for Patient and Public Involvement in Health is also abolished and replaced by these arrangements. Essentially, this seems to be a decentralisation of service user influence, which it is hoped will give each local involvement network a more local and therefore relevant focus, in line with current Government policy.

The Act also deals with such diverse subjects as electoral arrangements, boundary changes and the role of parishes, to name a few.

## Work and Families Act 2006

This Act is concerned with maternity and paternity leave, flexible working, redundancy payments and annual leave. It is not specifically concerned with direct care work in the health and social care field but may be of passing interest. We recommend further study if relevant, but two of the Act's main objectives are to:

O   Extend the maximum period of statutory maternity pay, maternity allowance and statutory adoption pay from 26 weeks to 52 weeks.

O   Introduce a scheme to entitle certain employees (usually fathers) to take leave to care for a child and receive pay if they meet certain conditions.

## Sustainable Communities Act 2007
Territorial extent: England and Wales

This Act received Royal Assent on 23rd October 2007.

This Act does not talk about issues of direct care. However, it is part of the government's agenda to encourage more public participation in local communities, to make them more "sustainable" socially, economically and environmentally. It is worth a closer look if the reader is involved in community development work or environmental issues.

## Welfare Reform Act 2007

This Act received Royal Assent on 3$^{rd}$ May 2007.

This Act brings changes to a number of welfare benefits. The underlying agenda is to promote greater social responsibility and reduce the perceived dependency culture thought to stem from the benefits system. Another stated aim of this legislation is to increase employment for single mothers and people over 50.

The Reforms

○ Incapacity benefit and Income Support are replaced by the new Employment and Support Allowance (ESA). ESA is accompanied by a new Personal Capacity Assessment which assesses a person's entitlement and the level of support they would need to get back into work. People deemed able to work must attend interviews and with help, put together a work focused action plan.

○ Housing Benefit gets a shake up: benefits will be paid direct to claimants rather than direct to landlords. Some charity organisations and other commentators see this as a potential problem for certain vulnerable groups, such as drug users and others who may find the additional responsibility daunting.

○ The Local Housing Allowance system will now be applied to the whole private rented sector.

○ There will be Housing Benefit sanctions applied to people who don't change their behaviour following eviction for anti social behaviour.

○ New powers will allow better sharing of information between the Department of Work and Pensions and local authorities to increase the take up of social security benefits.

○ There are other amendments to the social security system and some provisions relating to compensation for vaccine damage.

It must be said that this is a very brief summary of some major changes in benefits provision. Undoubtedly, if the reader is involved in benefits advocacy, they should study the Act and regulations in greater depth.

## Criminal Justice and Immigration Bill 2007/2008
Territorial Extent: UK Wide

This Bill proposes new powers to deal with violent and anti social behaviour and clarify sentencing issues.

o   Makes victims needs central to the role of the criminal justice system
o   Tougher response when offenders fail to appear in court
o   New powers to tackle violent and anti social behaviour, including clearer sentencing
o   New offence relating to violent pornography
o   Generic Community sentence for young offenders
o   Addresses issues that can cause sentences to be overturned, resulting in offenders being released
o   Brings compensation for wrongful imprisonment into line with that paid to victims

Clearly this Bill, if passed through Parliament and enacted in full, will address a number of public concerns around anti-social behaviour and the perceived inadequacies in the disposal of sentences.

 **In Summary**

One of the reasons that care staff need to have an understanding of the legal framework and a wide range of legislation is because we work with people!  Not only is there a wide range of legislation specific to health and social care, but all people live within a legal framework. This means we not only need to understand sector specific legislation, but also the legislation which applies generally to all British citizens.

# ( 13 ) STAFF WORKING IN WALES

At present, the primary legislation (Acts of Parliament) that relates to Wales is very similar to legislation that relates to England. However, there could be increased divergence as the Welsh Assembly starts to introduce its own Assembly Measures (Acts that relate to Wales only).

This chapter will cover:

O   Government of Wales Act 2006
O   Commissioner for Older People (Wales) Act 2006
O   Care Standards Act 2000

and associated policy and guidance

## Government of Wales Act 2006

Through this Act the recommendations of the 2005 White Paper "Better Government for Wales" have been introduced. As a result, the Welsh Assembly Government and the National Assembly have two routes by which the legislative powers of the National Assembly can be extended.

The new routes could be used in any or all of the 12 devolved 'fields'. The devolved fields include heath (and health matters), housing and education.

When the National Assembly uses these new routes, legislation introduced by the National Assembly will be termed an Assembly Measure.

## Commissioner for Older People (Wales) Act 2006

This Act creates the office of Commissioner for Older People in Wales or Comisiynydd Pobl Hyn Cymru. The Commissioners role includes:

O  promote awareness of the interests of older people in Wales

O  act to eliminate discrimination against older people in Wales and promote opportunities

O  review the adequacy and effectiveness of law affecting the well being of older people in Wales

O  review complaints and whistle blowing procedures of statutory (public) bodies that provide services for older people

### Policy and Guidance

The Assembly Government has been active in developing policies and guidance that relate to health and community care.

Policy and guidance are not generally discussed in this book. Therefore what follows is brief.

## Building for the Future: A White Paper for Wales 1999

This White Paper outlines the Welsh Assembly Governments' aspiration for social care. It includes chapters on:

O   Improving services

O   Interagency working

O   Regulating services

O   Raising standards in the social care workforce

O   Children's services

O   Adult services

## In Safe Hands: Implementing Adult Protection Procedures in Wales 2000

This is guidance issued under section 7 of the Local Authority Social Services Act 1970.

It highlights the need for written policy and procedures, the importance of interagency working and applying an assertive response to allegations of abuse. The document discusses options for local authorities given that some unitary authorities are relatively small and may not have specialist adult protection teams.

## Care Standards Act 2000

As referred to already it is the implementation of legislation that is decided by the Welsh Assembly Government.

Provider services of health and social care are registered and inspected by the Care Standards Inspectorate for Wales (CSIW). The Regulations – The Care Homes (Wales) Regulations 2002 and the National Minimum Standards for the respective services are generated by the Welsh Assembly Government.

The Care Council for Wales (Cyngor Gofal Cymru) is the body responsible for raising standards in the social care workforce by promoting training and is also responsible for compiling and maintaining a register of staff who work in social care.

## Other Policy Developments

Before devolution occurred Wales already had various national strategies in place. These included the All Wales Strategy in respect of people with learning disabilities and the mental health strategy Mental Illness Services: A Strategy for Wales. The establishment of the Welsh Assembly will lead to these being reviewed and updated as necessary.

Additionally the Welsh Assembly Government has developed the Strategy for Older People in Wales. This seeks to address issues of age discrimination and social exclusion encountered by older people as well as outlining aspirations for improvements in health and social care.

### In Summary

The Welsh Assembly Government has indicated it's desire for increased autonomy in terms of deciding on the delivery of health and social care. It is therefore a real possibility that the provision of health and social care in Wales will become increasingly distinctive and based on the aspirations of the people of Wales

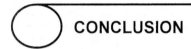

# CONCLUSION

It is seen as increasingly important that all staff are aware of the law that is relevant to them.

As can be seen from this brief guide there are many Acts of Parliament and regulations that could be relevant for any one service.

Knowledge of the law is not an end in itself, it just informs us where the boundaries of our work lie. We then need to work effectively, consistently and fairly within these legal boundaries. Hence it is equally important for staff to be familiar with their organisation's policies and procedures.

As knowledge of the law increases, especially in the area of anti-oppressive legislation and rights, then people will become increasingly likely to invoke these rights. This is to be welcomed. If over time expectations and standards rise then it will be for the benefit of all.

# REFERENCES

Department of Health (2000) *No Secrets: Guidance on Developing and Implementing Multi-Agency Policies and Procedures to Protect Vulnerable Adults from Abuse* (London) Department of Health

HMSO (2000) *Explanatory Notes to the Care Standards Act 2000* (Internet) HMSO.

Home Office (2000) *Domestic Violence - Break the Chain. Multi-Agency Guidance for Addressing Domestic Violence* (Internet) Home Office.

Home Office (2004) *Guidance to the Sexual Offences Act 2004*, (Internet) Home Office

Winchester, R. (2000) Pressure builds to revamp consent laws in wake of failed rape charge. *Community Care* 3-9 February.

Wragg, T. (1995) *Family Law in a Nutshell.* Sweet and Maxwell, London.

# NVQ UNIT INDEX

**National Occupational Standards for Health and Social Care**

This index details all the NVQ units potentially relevant to work in adult services. Details are provided on where to find the legal knowledge for the units in this book.

**NB:** Chapter 12 is potentially relevant to all units depending on a worker's role. Chapter 13 is relevant to all candidates working in Wales. These two chapters are therefore not specifically covered in this index.

## Level Two Units

| Unit | Covered in the following chapters of this book | Page Numbers |
|------|-----------------------------------------------|--------------|
| HSC 21 | 4, 5 and 6 | 21 to 42 |
| HSC22 | 4, 5, 6 and 7 | 21 to 54 |
| HSC23 | 4, 5 and 6 | 21 to 42 |
| HSC24 | 4, 5, 6, 7 and 9 | 21 to 54 and 61 to 80 |
| HSC25 | 6 | 39 to 42 |
| HSC26 | 4, 5 and 6 | 21 to 42 |
| HSC27 | 4, 5, 6 and 7 | 21 to 54 |
| HSC28 | 4, 5, 6 and 7 | 21 to 54 |
| HSC29 | 4, 5, 6 and 7 | 21 to 54 |
| HSC210 | 4, 5, 6 and 7 | 21 to 54 |
| HSC211 | 4, 5, 6 and 7 | 21 to 54 |
| HSC212 | 4, 5, 6 and 7 | 21 to 54 |
| HSC213 | 4, 5, 6 and 7 | 21 to 54 |
| HSC214 | 4, 5, 6 and 7 | 21 to 54 |
| HSC215 | 4, 5, 6 and 7 | 21 to 54 |
| HSC216 | 4, 5, 6 and 7 | 21 to 54 |
| HSC217 | 7 | 43 to 54 |
| HSC218 | 4, 5, 6 and 7 | 21 to 54 |
| HSC219 | 4, 5, 6 and 7 | 21 to 54 |
| HSC220 | 7 | 43 to 54 |
| HSC223 | 4, 5, 6 and 7 | 21 to 54 |
| HSC224 | 4, 5 and 6 | 21 to 42 |
| HSC225 | 4, 5, 6 and 7 | 21 to 54 |
| HSC226 | 4, 5 and 6 | 21 to 42 |
| HSC227 | 4, 5, 6 and 7 | 21 to 54 |
| HSC228 | 4, 5, 6 and 7 | 21 to 54 |

| Unit | Covered in the following chapters of this book | Page Numbers |
|---|---|---|
| HSC229 | 4, 5, 6 and 7 | 21 to 54 |
| HSC230 | 7 | 43 to 54 |
| HSC233 | 7 | 43 to 54 |
| HSC234 | 4, 5, 6, 10 and 11 | 21 to 42 and 81 to 101 |
| HSC235 | 4, 5, 6 and 7 | 21 to 54 |
| HSC239 | 4, 5, 6 and 7 | 21 to 54 |
| HSC240 | 4, 5, 6 and 7 | 21 to 54 |
| HSC241 | 4, 5 and 6 | 21 to 42 |
| HSC242 | 4, 5 and 6 | 21 to 42 |
| HSC243 | 7 | 43 to 54 |
| HSC244 | 4, 5, 6 and 7 | 21 to 54 |
| HSC245 | 4, 5, 6 and 7 | 21 to 54 |
| HSC246 | 6 and 7 | 39 to 54 |

## Level Three Units (Core and Optional – Adults)

| Unit | Covered in the following chapters of this book | Page Numbers |
|---|---|---|
| HSC31 | 6 | 39 to 42 |
| HSC32 | 4, 5, 6 and 7 | 21 to 54 |
| HSC33 | 4 and 5 | 21 to 37 |
| HSC35 | 4, 5, 6, 7, 8 and 9 | 21 to 80 |
| HSC328 | 4, 5, 6 and 7 | 21 to 54 |
| HSC329 | 4, 5, 6, 7 and 9 | 21 to 54 and 61 to 80 |
| HSC330 | 4, 5, 6, 7, 9, 10 and 11 | 21 to 54 and 61 to 101 |
| HSC331 | 4, 5, 6 and 7 | 21 to 54 |
| HSC332 | 4, 5, 6 and 7 | 21 to 54 |
| HSC333 | 4, 5, 6 and 9 | 21 to 42 and 61 to 80 |
| HSC334 | 4, 5, 6 and 9 | 21 to 42 and 61 to 80 |
| HSC335 | 4, 5, 6 and 9 | 21 to 42 and 61 to 80 |
| HSC337 | 4, 5, 6 and 7 | 21 to 54 |

## Level Three Units (Generic Optional Units)

| Unit | Covered in the following chapters of this book | Page Numbers |
|---|---|---|
| HSC343 | 4, 5, 6 and 7 | 21 to 54 |
| HSC344 | 4, 5, 6 and 7 | 21 to 54 |
| HSC345 | 4, 5, 6 and 7 | 21 to 54 |
| HSC346 | 4, 5, 6 and 7 | 21 to 54 |
| HSC347 | 4, 5, 6 and 7 | 21 to 54 |
| HSC348 | 4, 5, 6 and 7 | 21 to 54 |
| HSC349 | 4, 5, 6, 7 and 10 | 21 to 54 and 81 to 95 |
| HSC350 | 4, 5, 6 and 7 | 21 to 54 |
| HSC351 | 4, 5, 6 and 7 | 21 to 54 |
| HSC352 | 4, 5, 6 and 7 | 21 to 54 |
| HSC356 | 4, 5, 6 and 7 | 21 to 54 |
| HSC360 | 7 | 43 to 54 |
| HSC361 | 7 | 43 to 54 |
| HSC364 | 10 | 81 to 95 |
| HSC366 | 4, 5, 6 and 7 | 21 to 54 |
| HSC367 | 4, 5 and 6 | 21 to 42 |
| HSC368 | 4, 5 and 6 | 21 to 42 |
| HSC369 | 4, 5, 6 and 7 | 21 to 54 |
| HSC370 | 4, 5, 6 and 7 | 21 to 54 |
| HSC371 | 4, 5, 6 and 7 | 21 to 54 |
| HSC372 | 4, 5, 6 and 7 | 21 to 54 |
| HSC373 | 4, 5, 6 and 7 | 21 to 54 |
| HSC375 | 7 and 10 | 43 to 54 and 81 to 95 |
| HSC379 | 7 and 10 | 43 to 54 and 81 to 95 |
| HSC382 | 4, 5, 6 and 7 | 21 to 54 |
| HSC383 | 4, 5, 6 and 7 | 21 to 54 |
| HSC384 | 4, 5 and 6 | 21 to 42 |
| HSC385 | 4, 5, 6 and 7 | 21 to 54 |
| HSC387 | 4, 5, 6, 7 and 10 | 21 to 54 and 81 to 95 |
| HSC388 | 4, 5, 6 and 7 | 21 to 54 |
| HSC389 | 4, 5, 6, 7 and 9 | 21 to 54 and |
| HSC392 | 10 and 11 | 81 to 101 |
| HSC393 | 4, 5, 6 and 7 | 21 to 54 |
| HSC394 | 4, 5, 6, 7 and 9 | 21 to 54 and |
| HSC395 | 4, 5, 6, 7 and 9 | 21 to 54 and |
| HSC396 | 10 | 81 to 95 |
| HSC397 | 10 | 81 to 95 |
| HSC398 | 4, 5, 6, 7 and 9 | 21 to 54 and |
| HSC3100 | 4, 5, 6 and 7 | 21 to 54 |

| Unit | Covered in the following chapters of this book | Page Numbers |
|---|---|---|
| HSC3101 | 4, 5, 6, 7 and 10 | 21 to 54 and 81 to 95 |
| HSC3102 | 4, 5, 6, 7 and 10 | 21 to 54 and 81 to 95 |
| HSC3103 | 4, 5, 6 and 7 | 21 to 54 |
| HSC3109 | 10 and 11 | 81 to 101 |
| HSC3110 | 4, 5, 6 and 7 | 21 to 54 |

## Level Three Units (Additional)

| Unit | Covered in the following chapters of this book | Page Numbers |
|---|---|---|
| HSC3111 | 4, 5, 6 and 7 | 21 to 54 |
| HSC3112 | 4, 5, 6, 7 and 10 | 21 to 54 and 81 to 95 |
| HSC3114 | 4, 5, 6 and 7 | 21 to 54 |
| HSC3115 | 4, 5, 6, 7 and 9 | 21 to 54 and 61 to 80 |
| HSC3116 | 4, 5 and 6 | 21 to 42 |
| HSC3117 | 7 | 43 to 54 |
| HSC3118 | 7 | 43 to 54 |
| HSC3119 | 4, 5, 10 and 11 | 21 to 37 and 81 to 101 |
| HSC3121 | 4, 5, 6, 7 and 10 | 21 to 54 and 81 to 95 |

## Level Four Units (Core and Optional – Adults)

| Unit | Covered in the following sections of this book | Page Numbers |
|---|---|---|
| HSC41 | 4, 5, 6 and 9 | 21 to 42 and 61 to 80 |
| HSC42 | 4, 5, 6, 7 and 9 | 21 to 54 and 61 to 80 |
| HSC43 | 4, 5 ,6 and 11 | 21 to 42 and 97 to 101 |
| HSC45 | 4, 5, 6, 7, 9, 10 and 11 | 21 to 54 and 61 to 101 |
| HSC410 | 6 and 10 | 39 to 42 and 81 to 95 |
| HSC411 | 9, 10 and 11 | 61 to 101 |
| HSC412 | 10 | 81 to 95 |

## Level Four Units (Generic Optional Units)

| Unit | Covered in the following sections of this book | Page Numbers |
|---|---|---|
| HSC413 | 4, 5, 6, 7, 9 and 10 | 21 to 54 and 61 to 95 |
| HSC414 | 4, 5, 6 and 7 | 21 to 54 |
| HSC415 | 4, 5, 6, 7, 9, 10 and 11 | 21 to 54 and 61 to 101 |
| HSC416 | 4, 5, 6, 7, 9, 10 and 11 | 21 to 54 |
| HSC417 | 10 and 11 | 81 to 101 |
| HSC418 | 6, 10 and 11 | 39 to 42 and 81 to 101 |
| HSC419 | 6 and others (dependent on role) | 39 to 42 |
| HSC420 | 7, 10 and 11 | 43 to 54 and 81 to 101 |
| HSC423 | 6, 7 and 9 | 39 to 54 and 61 to 80 |
| HSC425 | 4, 5, 6, 7 and 9 | 21 to 54 and 61 to 80 |
| HSC426 | 10 | 81 to 95 |
| HSC429 | 4, 5 and 6 | 21 to 42 |
| HSC430 | 4, 5, 6, 7 and 9 | 21 to 54 and 61 to 80 |
| HSC431 | 4, 5, 6, 7 and 9 | 21 to 54 and 61 to 80 |
| HSC433 | 4, 5, 6, 7, 9 and 11 | 21 to 54, 61 to 80 and 97 to 101 |
| HSC435 | 4, 5, 6, 10 and 11 | 21 to 42 and 81 to 101 |
| HSC436 | 11 | 97 to 101 |
| HSC446 | 6, 7, 10 and 11 | 39 to 54 and 81 to 101 |
| HSC449 | 10 and 11 | 81 to 101 |
| HSC550 | 4, 5, 6, 7 and 9 | 21 to 54 and 61 to 80 |
| HSC551 | 4, 5, 6, 7 and 9 | 21 to 54 and 61 to 80 |

# INDEX TO LEGISLATION